THE SIXTIES

A FIREFLY BOOK

Published by Firefly Books Ltd. 2018

First printing

Publisher Cataloging-in-Publication Data (U.S.)

Library of Congress Control Number: 2018930202

Library and Archives Canada Cataloguing in Publication

Hattstein, Markus, author
    The sixties : freedom, change and revolution / Markus
Hattstein, Christoph Marx.
Includes index.
ISBN 978-0-228-10129-1 (softcover)
    1. Nineteen sixties. 2. Nineteen sixties--Pictorial works.
3. Nineteen sixties--Political aspects. 4. Nineteen sixties--Social
aspects. 5. Protest movements--History--20th century. 6. Civil rights
movements--History--20th century. 7. Counterculture--History--20th
century. 8. Civilization--20th century. 9. History, Modern--20th
century. I. Marx, Christoph, author II. Title.
CB425.H38 2018   909.82'6   C2018-900179-8

Published in the United States by	Published in Canada by
Firefly Books (U.S.) Inc.	Firefly Books Ltd.
P.O. Box 1338, Ellicott Station	50 Staples Avenue, Unit 1
Buffalo, New York 14205	Richmond Hill, Ontario L4B 0A7

Translation: Natalie Lewis

Printed in Canada

Markus Hattstein / Christoph Marx

THE SIXTIES

Freedom, Change and Revolution

FIREFLY BOOKS

CONTENTS

PREFACE

the sixties are an era *of upheaval, liberation movements, and emancipation worldwide. This applies to all areas, from everyday life and culture to politics and social commitment. No decade from the Second World War until the present day is more characterized by dynamism, creative will, and the "utopia of feasibility" than the 1960s. Particularly in Africa, Latin America, and parts of Asia, the 1960s bring self-liberation and autonomy, while student protests and spontaneous movements in the Western industrial nations break up outdated traditions and set in motion liberalizations that continue to shape our lives today. A rebellious young generation is changing the world with its music, its ways of life, and its utopias. Many of these things culminate in the magical year of 1968, but as a whole, the 1960s are an excited and exciting, colorful and diverse, experimental and explosive decade.*

THE SIXTIES PHENOMENON

For many cultures, not only for the West, the 1960s are connected to movement and social unrest that finds expression in liberation struggles, the independence of many countries, modernization from top to bottom, progress in science and technology, protest marches, civil rights and emancipation movements, campaigns and imaginative activism. For Africa, for example, the "African Year" 1960 (and its consequences) is probably the most important turning point in its recent history and the beginning of the end of traditional colonialism. In the Western world, social pluralism gains ground in a strident and imaginative way in all areas of culture and everyday life, leading to the establishment of civil society as we know it today. The 1960s are rightly regarded as a "trigger" for many things that have since become part of the foundation of modern democratic societies, such as respect for and protection of minorities, equal rights for homosexuals and alternative ways of living, but also the presence and coexistence of very different preferences in music, clothing, culture, and lifestyle.

In many ways, the 1960s generation see themselves in stark contrast to the "stuffy" and culturally narrow-minded 1950s. Particularly the youth protest movements and minority civil rights activists strive toward a provocative disruption. While this may be true in many areas, this view also serves as a myth of self-legitimization, as some movements began in the 1950s but only fully evolved in the dynamic climate of the 1960s. Just think of the influence of Egyptian president Nasser and Pan-Arabism in the Middle East, the boycott movements of African-Americans, Maoism in China, the cultural thaw during

A student talks to a military policeman in Berkeley in 1964.

the Khrushchev era in the Eastern Bloc, or the fight against rearmament and the Easter peace marches in West Germany.

Nevertheless, there is a certain "spirit of the 60s" that expresses itself not only in these goals, but also in certain forms of action and types of engagement. Particularly in Africa and Latin America, these are militant, primarily Marxist-socialist, liberation movements, determined to fight for power. In the West, extra-parliamentary and primarily student action groups dominate the scene with protest marches, posters, and pamphlets, but also with exciting events such as blockades, sit-ins, building occupation events and legendary rock concerts. They orchestrate the spontaneous "power of the street" and feel connected to an anti-authoritarian, free socialism with anarchist characteristics. In hindsight, one may criticize many aspects of the era as naive and half-baked, but the power and energy with which all these movements thrust themselves forward, with some even prepared to use violence, are astounding. From today's perspective, the 1960s appear overly idealistic, not least because they were the last period characterized by an unbroken optimism about progress and an undaunted faith in the realization of change in all areas of life. But not all modernizations were brought about peacefully or from the bottom up.

WHAT IS THE AIM OF THIS BOOK?

It is precisely this "spirit of the 60s" that the book seeks to capture in highlights and also to present in its greater context. The book therefore intentionally focuses on struggles for freedom and independence, student protests, and civil rights movements, but also on the most important cultural revolutions and musical events, from the Beatles to Woodstock, as well as scientific and technological innovations, culminating in the moon landing as well as in medical advancements like organ transplants. These awakenings and changes, and their respective forms of action and expression, with their optimistic or even revolutionary impetus, are described in detail. In addition to the most important and consequential developments of the 1960s, marginal incidents — like hippie communes in the USA or the Indonesian girl group Dara Puspita — are portrayed insofar as they relate to the spirit of the decade.

This book is not a mere chronicle tracing the sequence of major historical events in the 1960s, and therefore many "negative" or reactionary developments, which also took place during this contradictory decade, are omitted. Hence, the numerous ethnic and religious conflicts are missing, and only two decisive wars are taken into account: the civil war during the Congo crisis, because it promoted the decolonization of Africa, and especially the Vietnam War, because it uniquely determines our understanding of "proxy wars" with the highest civilian casualties to this day, and also because it provoked tremendous waves of protest. The book deliberately leaves out events like the military coup in what is today Myanmar in 1962, which has left the country isolated until the present day; the long-standing military dictatorship in Brazil; or the regimes of Marcos in the Philippines and Mobutu in Zaire, established in 1964–65. This list could go on.

Consequently, this book shows how the social upheaval and dynamic spirit of the often cherished, but also much maligned 1960s evolved in many countries around the world — and what it managed to achieve.

Markus Hattstein

Visitors to the "James Bond Club" in Jakarta in modern clothing, 1967.

the african year

18 states gain their independence

While colonized countries in Asia gained their independence mostly through violent struggle in the years right after the Second World War, the old colonial powers continued to hold on to their control over Africa. It was not until the mid-1950s that the pressure of the protesting colonies caused them to rethink the situation. After securing their economic privileges, Great Britain and France plan a peaceful transition of power to local African administrations. They appoint the leading figures of independence movements as new heads of government — often men they had previously imprisoned or exiled — and finally give them power. However, they retain their influence on economic aid, technical know-how, and the arms trade.

After Ghana and Guinea led the way in 1957–58, a total of 18 African countries gain their independence between January and November 1960: Cameroon, Togo, Madagascar, Somalia (which was initially two countries), the Democratic Republic of the Congo, Benin, Niger, Burkina Faso, Ivory Coast, Chad, the Central African Republic, the Republic of the Congo, Gabon, Senegal, Mali, Nigeria, and Mauritania.

In the years leading up to 1968, another 16 African countries achieve independence — indeed, one can speak of the 1960s as the "African Decade."

There are distinguished figures and wise statesmen among the black independence leaders who soon gain an international reputation and give the African continent a proud and autonomous voice. But there are also those who turn out to be dictators or shameless "kleptocrats." African parties are dominated by individual ethnicities or tribes, and in many countries governments are controlled by a single political party. The rivalry between different ethnic groups remains a source of conflict, yet some countries soon experience considerable progress in literacy as well as in basic medical care and social well-being.

However, in several African countries, the first governments are soon overthrown by brutal power players, sometimes with the support of the military.

In the Central African Republic, for example, President David Dacko is overthrown in 1966 by his cousin Jean-Bédel Bokassa, who establishes one of the most bizarre terror regimes of the 20th century and eventually crowns himself Emperor Bokassa I. France, as the former colonial power in the region, first profits from Bokassa's expensive coronation, which costs several million dollars, and then brings Dacko back to power in 1979.

Citizens of the Congo celebrate their country's independence on July 1, 1960.

1960

women in politics

The gradual progress of gender equality

Although there have been female monarchs and sovereigns in every era, it has long been a popular prejudice in civil society that "rough politics" are not suitable for the "weaker sex," but are purely a "man's thing." It is not until 1960 that the world's first female head of government is elected: in Sri Lanka, Sirimavo Bandaranaike succeeds her husband, who was murdered the year before.

By the end of the decade, two more women follow: Indira Gandhi in India in 1966, and Golda Meir in Israel 1969; Meir had previously become the first female foreign minister of a democratic country in 1956. All three of them also hold ministerial offices several times during their careers, rule with an iron fist, and leave no doubts about their leadership skills.

Although female politicians have held office several times in socialist countries, and even in the United States the first woman joined the cabinet as early as 1933, Western European countries are still having a hard time dealing with female leadership in the 1960s. The proportion of women in parliament remains below 10% until the early 1970s, and their political efforts are regularly ridiculed in the press with sarcastic or even overtly sexist comments.

In 1961 Elisabeth Schwarzhaupt is the first woman to be nominated as a government minister in the Federal Republic of Germany. The Ministry of Health is created especially for her because her male colleagues regard her as unfit for other offices, since she cannot "hold her drink." Chancellor Konrad Adenauer's reaction is typical: "What are we supposed to do with a woman in the cabinet? Now we can no longer speak so openly!" The men fear female intrusion into "their" domain.

The outlook for Germany's neighbors is not much better: France briefly has a female government minister in 1947–48, but the next does not follow until 1974. Great Britain receives its first female cabinet member in 1964, and Austria follows in 1966, while it takes until the 1970s in the Netherlands and Italy. In Switzerland, Portugal, and Liechtenstein, women still do not even have the right to vote in the 1960s. However, the pioneering women in higher politics, who initially only hold "soft" ministries — such as health, welfare, family, and youth — know how to succeed, do a competent job, and mostly counter criticism and rude harassment with professional authority. Power relations start to change by the mid-1970s, but it is not until 1979 that Margaret Thatcher is elected as British prime minister, becoming the first female prime minister in Europe. She goes down in history as the "Iron Lady," demonstrating outstanding determination and leadership skills.

Sirimavo Bandaranaike gives an election speech on February 18, 1960.

1960 USA

the birth control pill

Women take family planning into their own hands

A drug named "Enovid" is officially approved. This brief and simple announcement, given by the U.S. Food and Drug Administration on May 9, 1960, is the breakthrough of perhaps the most important scientific development of the 20th century: the birth control pill, which guarantees nearly 100% protection against pregnancy.

For chemists, this was the preliminary conclusion of decades-long research work, from the production of artificial pregnancy hormones to the completion of a hormone compound, which would give the body the impression of being permanently pregnant.

This medical achievement radically questions established world-views and conservative moral concepts. Pregnancies are now no longer a matter of course, but something that can be actively prevented. What a revolution! The outcry in conservative circles, especially in the church, is huge. People fear the general decline of social conventions and sexual morality. In an encyclical Pope Paul VI denounces the pill as a sin, maintaining that the sexual act should only serve the purpose of "giving life." (To this day, the Catholic Church officially rejects the pill.)

Nevertheless, the success of oral contraceptives is unstoppable — despite the fact that some of the side effects in the first few years are quite dangerous. At first, the pill is only prescribed to married couples, but by the end of the 1960s, more and more women are swallowing these small pills. By the mid-1970s, three-quarters of the 19-year-olds in the U.S. have already had experience with the pill.

The pill allows women to independently take control of family planning. Women's new freedom to consciously decide whether or not to have children, not only changes understandings of sexuality, but also has a major impact on women's emancipation in almost all areas of society. It opens up opportunities for women to take up leading positions in all career fields, as it is now less likely that they will be torn from their professional lives by an unwanted pregnancy.

Twenty birth control pills for one month.

nouvelle vague

The dawn of a new cinema

Michel, a young car thief, kills a policeman and flees to Paris. There he tries to persuade his girlfriend, Patricia, to escape with him to Rome. But she wants to stay in Paris. When the police discover them, Patricia has to make a fateful choice: love or betrayal.

The 1960 film *Breathless* tells a classic, quite commonplace story of love and gangsters. Yet this movie would change the world of cinema forever, because what the up-and-coming filmmaker Jean-Luc Godard makes of this plot signifies a break with technical and narrative cinema conventions and a turning point in film history. Instead of filming in the studio, he shoots with a light, handheld camera directly on location for the first time, either in a room or on the street. More than a quarter of his story is set in a hotel room, where Michel and Patricia argue, philosophize, and sleep together. The existentialist Godard stages this love relationship with an intimate, lifelike touch and develops an entirely new, unconventional narrative style with fast jump cuts.

The film is an immediate success and becomes the pioneer of the so-called Nouvelle Vague ("New Wave"), which strives to make more individual, artistic films. A New Wave film is supposed to be based on the vision of the director who transforms from a mere translator of the script into the one who designs all the film's artistry. Thus a film should also mirror the personality of the director. Together with François Truffaut, Claude Chabrol, and Éric Rohmer, Godard revolutionizes European filmmaking in the 1960s. The Nouvelle Vague establishes cinema as an independent art form alongside literature and art.

Jean-Paul Belmondo and Jean Seberg in Jean-Luc Godard's film Breathless.

1960

the congo crisis

The difficult path to democracy

Of all African countries the Congo experienced the harshest colonial rule. Until 1908, the country had been under rule by the Belgian king Leopold II, who enslaved the inhabitants and forced them to work on his rubber plantations. His "Congo Atrocities" cost 10 million lives, and subsequent rule by the Belgian state, which forbids any type of political activity, is also gruesome, abruptly abandoning the country in complete chaos after escalating riots in 1959.

About 100 fringe parties compete in the country's first democratic elections. In the end, the charismatic candidate Patrice Lumumba wins and becomes the first premier. The independence celebrations begin with an outright scandal: Lumumba interrupts the Belgian king Baudouin during his address lauding the "civilized achievements" made under colonial rule and gives an emotional speech on the issue of slavery.

Lumumba is now considered an "enemy of the whites." His program of political union and plans to nationalize the Congo's mines, mineral resources, and agricultural products is branded as "communism" by the former economic powers, Belgium and the USA, and Lumumba is even condemned as "Satan." U.S. intelligence agencies suggest assassinating Lumumba, who is seeking help from the Soviets, and King Baudouin is in the know. Both countries support Lumumba's enemy Moïse Tshombe in organizing the secession of the diamond-rich province of Katanga and encourage his former ally and army chief of staff, Joseph Mobutu, to revolt.

The deposed Lumumba flees from Kinshasa but is captured by Mobutu and handed over to Tshombe, who has Lumumba and two of his allies tortured and killed. His corpse is dismembered, doused with acid, and burned. After securing further economic concessions for themselves, Belgium and the USA support Mobutu, who later renames himself Mobutu Sese Seko and changes the name of the state to Zaire, which is to become one of the most brutal "kleptocratic regimes" in Africa and where an increasingly absurd personality cult for Mobutu endures until 1997.

The Congo remains in turmoil. The civil war over the secession of the southern province of Katanga, in which UN troops and mercenaries intervene, lasts until 1963.

Soon after his death, however, Lumumba is resurrected as an incorruptible hero and martyr who fought for freedom and against colonialism in Africa.

The ever-elegantly dressed prime minister of the Congo, Patrice Lumumba, arrives in New York on July 27, 1960, to negotiate with the UN on aid for his country.

television becomes a mass medium

The first televised presidential debate in history

October 7, 1960. The political race between John F. Kennedy and Richard Nixon is heading towards the finish line. For the first time, two candidates are fighting for voter support on TV.

The first televised presidential debate in U.S. history gives Kennedy a decisive advantage. For while the youthful, smiling John F. Kennedy seems relaxed, confident, and dynamic, Nixon looks tense and pale in his ill-fitting gray suit. Beads of sweat are clearly visible on his forehead. According to a survey, voters who listen to the debate on the radio give Nixon much higher approval ratings than Kennedy.

But Kennedy's telegenic charisma convinces the television audience, and many people are later convinced that this TV appearance secured the decisive votes that led to Kennedy's victory.

The rise of television as a new mass medium in the 1960s certainly also changes the democratic decision-making process in Western democracies. Following in the footsteps of the U.S., the share of households in Europe with a television set also increases to more than 70% between 1960 and 1970. And the politicians like to play along: They quickly realize that political messages can be spread much more effectively via the new "distraction medium" — television — instead of relying solely on newspapers and radio. Media-friendly presence and rhetoric become increasingly important. Kennedy becomes a role model for many Western politicians — such as Willy Brandt in Germany — as he involves his family and private life in the election campaign in order to boost his public appeal.

However, television serves more than just politics. The young rebels of the 1960s attract media attention with spectacular radical action, teach-ins, and sit-ins, thus reaching a broad audience.

In this way, the 1960s are the starting point for the politics of television images, which have become self-evident today, making a political career without these images almost unthinkable.

Passersby standing in front of a store window watching a speech by presidential candidate John F. Kennedy, October 1960.

YOUNG BROS
TV

a new frontier

The dawn of the Kennedy era

The excitement is boundless. On the way to an election campaign in New York, John F. Kennedy and his wife enjoy the celebration in their open cabriolet. The crowd waves posters emblazoned with slogans like "The Man for the 60s" and applauds the young couple with enthusiastic cheers.

Like no other politician, John F. Kennedy embodies the hope of young Americans for political renewal. In his acceptance speech at the 1960 Democratic National Convention, he says "We stand today on the edge of a New Frontier — the frontier of the 1960s, a frontier of unknown opportunities and perils, a frontier of unfulfilled hopes and threats." In this sense, he wants to create a fairer country, specifically by reforming the health care and educational systems, by combating poverty, and, above all, by ending discrimination against African-Americans. Kennedy's political aim of breaking into the modern era is also perfectly embodied in the appearance and demeanor of his wife. When Kennedy is elected the 35th President of the United States in January 1961, Jacqueline brings style and culture to the White House. First, she modernizes the interior of the presidential residence in a media-savvy way and then she organizes art exhibitions and meetings with the country's leading intellectuals. Her elegant appearance has a mass impact: Jackie's style sets fashion trends, and her straight-cut dresses and famous pillbox hats are copied throughout the Western world. She stands for the look of a new generation that wants to shatter current aesthetic conventions.

The Kennedys embody the emerging enthusiasm for change among millions of people in the early 1960s — and not only in the U.S. They represent an open-minded and modern superpower. What gives hope to some is, however, a political and social affront to others. Conservative conformism prevails in the U.S. and racial marginalization is still part of everyday life. Even in universities, tradition and docile obedience are regarded as virtues. Yet the young people are starting to ask critical questions, thereby indirectly following the call of Kennedy's inauguration speech: "Ask not what your country can do for you — ask what you can do for your country."

This new spirit of optimism, however, comes to an abrupt end when John F. Kennedy is assassinated in Dallas on November 22, 1963.

President John F. Kennedy with his wife, Jacqueline, in a convoy parading down 5th Avenue in New York.

1961

1961 SOVIET UNION

the first manned space flight

Yuri Gagarin fascinates the world

In the 1950s and 1960s, the Cold War between the super-powers also manifests itself as a struggle for dominance in space. Initially, the Soviets take the lead: On October 4, 1957, the first satellite, Sputnik 1, is launched into space, marking the beginning of the space age. Having relied on their techno-logical superiority, the U.S. has barely digested the "Sputnik shock" when the Soviets raise the bar only two months later by sending the first living creature, a female dog named Laika, into space on Sputnik 2. Thus they prove that living beings can be launched into space, a topic which had hitherto been contro-versial — although Laika dies from overheating after six hours in space.

In 1958, the U.S. launches its first human spaceflight program, Project Mercury, and the race begins. On both sides, rodents, dogs, pigs, squirrel monkeys, and rhesus macaques are the unnamed heroes of the early space flights. After two Soviet dogs survive their flight

on Sputnik 5 in August 1960, the U.S. sends the first ape, a chimpanzee named Ham, into space in January 1961. The chimp survives the flight and goes on to live in a zoo for another 22 years.

However, the Russians take the lead for the third time: On April 12, 1961, the 27-year-old Soviet Air Force colonel Yuri Gagarin becomes the first human being in space, orbiting the earth in 106 minutes and reporting live on the beauty of our blue planet. While the new U.S. President John F. Kennedy makes space flight a high national priority in a famous speech and announces landing an American on the moon as a major goal, Soviet Premier Khrushchev celebrates his triumph and hugs Gagarin like a mascot at public appearances.

Immediately elevated to the status of a "Hero of the Soviet Union," Gagarin, the humble, grounded son of a carpenter and a milkmaid, fulfills all the criteria of a working-class hero. Khrushchev sends him on a

propaganda tour of several continents. The "ambassador of peace" is welcomed enthusiastically in countries such as Austria, Great Britain, and India and meets the world's power players.

However, Gagarin does not handle the whole commotion very well. He does not want to be a mere poster child, and he takes part in other flight projects. In March 1968, he dies when his MiG crashes while on a training flight. The Soviet Union goes into national mourning, and his urn is buried at the Kremlin Wall. In many Eastern Bloc countries, streets, schools, and kindergartens soon bear his name, and his likeness often adorns stamps: Gagarin's pioneering achievements stand not only for technological progress — which is celebrated in all systems worldwide — but also as a symbol of the efficiency of the communist state system.

The moon is the next goal: there is no limit to space travel euphoria in the USSR after Gagarin's successful mission. Propaganda poster, c. 1962.

1961 USA

the peace corps

Ask not what your country can do for you …

The Peace Corps is one of the most visible and enduring symbols of the renaissance of hope in America that marked the Kennedy campaign and early years of his Administration. It began at 2 AM during an impromptu speech to students on the steps of the University of Michigan in what would later be called "the founding moment." A tired John F. Kennedy challenged the students to take up service in the Peace Corps for the greater good of all. "Ask not what your country can do for you," he said, "ask what you can do for your country." A challenge that Kennedy would pose to the entire nation at his inauguration.

Kennedy characterized the 1961 presidential campaign as "the most important … since 1933, mostly because of the problems which press upon the United States, and the opportunities that will be presented to us in the 1960s." Then he asked,

"How many of you who are going to be doctors, are willing to spend your days in Ghana? Technicians or engineers, how many of you are willing to work in the Foreign Service and spend your lives traveling around the world? On your willingness to contribute part of your life to this country, I think will depend the answer whether a free society can compete. I think it can! And I think Americans are willing to contribute. But the effort must be far greater than we have ever made in the past."

Kennedy signed the Peace Corps into being on March 1, 1961, shortly after he was sworn in as President. In the first few months over 10,000 applications were received. Future luminaries who served in the Peace Corps included: Paul Tsongas, former US senator, served in Ethiopia 1962-1964 and the West Indies 1967 to 1968; Paul Theroux, author, served in Malawi 1963 to 1965; Chris Matthews, journalist, served in Swaziland 1968 to 1970; Christopher Dodd, former US Senator, served in the Dominican Republic 1966 to 1968; and Lillian Carter, at 68 and mother of future President Jimmy Carter, served in India 1966 to 1968.

The Peace Corps offered Americans a way to help those less fortunate than themselves while changing the lives of the thousands of volunteers who served in the education, health care, agriculture, business and other programs in 74 countries. It also helped the United States meet the Cold War challenge by showing the Soviet Union that Americans were willing to sacrifice part of their lives for the good of others less fortunate than themselves.

The first members of the Peace Corps leave for overseas duty in Ghana.

cuba libre

Fidel Castro declares Cuba a communist state

There is something wildly romantic about the Cuban revolution under Fidel Castro, who lands on the island with 82 fighters at the end of 1956 and takes province after province, until he triumphantly succeeds in occupying Havana in January 1959.

At first, the revolution is fueled by the charisma of Fidel Castro and Che Guevara (see page 132), even while its direction is still unclear to those involved. An extensive agricultural reform drives the old upper class out of the country and upsets the U.S. After Cuba also nationalizes its banks and U.S. oil refineries, President Eisenhower instructs the CIA to overthrow Castro. However, the Cuban Revolutionary Army fends off the invasion at the Bay of Pigs in April 1961.

The Soviet leader Khrushchev realizes that this development is driving Cuba into the arms of the USSR. He quickly assures Cuba of generous economic aid, which Castro uses for education and literacy programs, improvements in medical care, and wage increases. It is precisely this policy that temporarily turns Cuba into a model for a liberated Latin America supported by undogmatic leftists all over the world, inspired by the revolutionary gestures of Castro and, above all, Guevara.

Under Soviet influence, Castro proclaims Cuba a "Socialist Republic" on December 2, 1961. The revolutionary party becomes the Communist Party of Cuba, and the economy is centralized. After the U.S. imposes a total economic embargo at the beginning of 1962, the local Cuban population fluctuates between revolutionary enthusiasm at mass rallies, despair over a scarcity economy, and cunning small-scale improvisations. Meanwhile, the world is headed for a menacing crisis over Cuba (see page 48).

Fidel Castro gives a speech in Revolution Square in Havana on May Day 1962.

the eichmann trial

The "banality of evil" shocks the world

In May 1960, a unit of the Mossad, Israel's secret service, kidnaps a worker named Ricardo Klement in a suburb of Buenos Aires and secretly takes him to Israel by plane. Many authorities, including the German foreign intelligence agency, the BND, are aware at this time that Ricardo Klement is in fact Adolf Eichmann, one of the major organizers of the Holocaust who has escaped to Argentina with the help of several organizations. During the Third Reich, Eichmann headed the Gestapo's Office of Jewish Affairs. In the occupied countries of Europe, his agency coordinated the gathering and deportation of Jews to extermination camps in the East with merciless efficiency.

Between April and December 1961, the Eichmann trial takes place in Jerusalem and becomes a global media event. The German press in particular reports nearly every day on the shocking court testimonies given by more than 100 Holocaust survivors, whose fate is revealed to the global public for the first time.

Eichmann, sitting in a bulletproof glass booth, seems willing and eager to testify. He deplores the murder of the Jews as a crime against humanity, for which he, in his opinion, bears no responsibility and of which he is therefore innocent in the legal sense. In the cross-examinations he presents himself as a minor functionary carrying out orders who was not involved in any sort of planning and he places full responsibility on his dead superiors Himmler and Heydrich.

The dull, insignificant impression which Eichmann strategically conveys leads the political theorist Hannah Arendt, who observes the trial, to coin the phrase "the banality of evil," describing the desk criminals of a murderous bureaucracy who efficiently execute the cruelest orders without resistance. She defines a type that exists in all terrorist regimes — but Eichmann was not one of them. Not only was he a participant in and a recorder of the notorious Wannsee Conference in 1942, but on tapes recorded in the 1950s and later published, he bragged about his deeds to like-minded people and expressed regret that he had not had time to send at least 11 or 12 million Jews to the extermination camps.

In December 1961, the court officially pronounces the only death sentence in the history of the state of Israel. Eichmann is hanged in June 1962.

The search for Holocaust perpetrators in hiding intensifies worldwide and succeeds in several spectacular cases. Particularly in Germany, young people begin to question the role their elders played in the Third Reich; thus far, most of them have claimed "not to have known anything" or to have merely been "small cogs in a big machine." The younger generation's distrust of the older generations will increase during the Auschwitz trials beginning in 1963 (see page 70).

Adolf Eichmann in the dock during his trial in 1961.

1961

the construction of the berlin wall

Berlin becomes the hot spot of the Cold War

The neighbors who live just a few yards away are suddenly beyond reach; shops and stores on the same street are as distant as the moon. What Berliners could hardly imagine, despite many dark rumors, becomes a grim reality between August 13 and 16, 1961: the communist GDR regime in East Berlin builds a wall around its sector, accurate to the meter, disregarding the organic course of the roads. The border is suddenly closed — commuters who have spent the night at a friend's place or at a hotel are no longer able to return to their neighborhoods; families are separated. There are dramatic scenes of escape and separation. When people start jumping out of the windows of houses in the East that border on sidewalks belonging to the West, the windows are barred or walled up.

Officially justified as a protection against aggression from the West, the Wall is actually the only way to stem the steadily increasing flow of refugees from the GDR into the West — and thus it ultimately confirms the moral bankruptcy of the oppressive GDR regime.

Just as it does for GDR citizens, the construction of the Wall through the middle of the city also demonstrates the powerlessness of West Berliners. While the mayor of West Berlin, Willy Brandt, writes flaming letters to President Kennedy urging him to take whatever countermeasures are necessary, the Western allied powers residing in the city react only four days after the beginning of the blockade — and then very cautiously and hesitantly. No one wants to risk starting a war over Berlin. Thus the construction of the Wall shows that both the Soviet Union and the U.S. are primarily concerned with safeguarding their own spheres of influence, and not with the establishment or preservation of a free society, as both sides continue to claim. The division of Berlin becomes a symbol for the division of the world.

Despite all the warnings, people constantly try to cross the border, even risking their lives. Dozens of attempts to escape through tunnels are documented. A total of at least 139 people are killed at the Berlin Wall — the last one in February 1989, just a few months before the fall of the Wall.

The driver of a BMW Isetta waves from West to East Berlin in the fall of 1961.

the shorter, the better

Mary Quant invents the miniskirt

Good riddance to long prissy circle skirts! Dancing freely also means freeing oneself from current fashion conventions. Anything that is superfluous or restricts free movement must go!

When Britain's bold designer Mary Quant takes up her scissors to shorten knee-length skirts by about four inches in her designer shop in Chelsea, she is not aware that she is creating a significant symbol of the rising women's liberation movement: the miniskirt. The publication of her designs in British *Vogue* in April 1962 immediately triggers a huge demand for Quant's miniskirts as well as turmoil in the fashion world.

Initially, Mary Quant simply wanted to create more practical leg space. It is not until conservative virtuecrats turn this "obscene rag" into a public scandal that the purchase of a simple piece of clothing unintentionally becomes a political statement for women's sexual freedom. Now more than ever: the shorter, the better.

As a stylish symbol of the era, the mini becomes a worldwide sensation. Quant's creations are neither expensive and elitist nor divisible into daytime and evening attire, but provide fresh, youthful everyday wear for the masses. Millions of women from all social backgrounds wear their skirts short now, and London surpasses Paris as the capital of avant-garde fashion.

Quant's boutique, which also sells the designer's patterned socks, PVC fashion, and later hot pants, becomes a fashion mecca. Her label moves away from the usual seasonal rhythm of launching fashion collections, preferring instead to present customers with new designs throughout the year, as soon as they are completed. This not only proves to be a positive marketing strategy for Quant, but also a further statement against the conventions of the international fashion industry.

Although fashion queen Coco Chanel complains about the knee being by far the most unattractive part of the female body, which therefore ought to be covered, even conservative circles gradually adjust to the new styles by the mid-1960s. Thus, Her Majesty Queen Elizabeth II honors Mary Quant's achievements in fashion with the Order of the British Empire, thereby showing off her own knee.

Mary Quant standing at her work table in one of her own miniskirt creations.

1962

the new superficiality

How pop art revolutionizes the art world

In the early 1960s, a young man by the name of Andy Warhola is about to take an important step. He has moved from provincial Pittsburgh to New York to start a career. He soon finds success as a graphic designer in advertising, but he wants more — he wants to become an artist, famous, and rich. The problem: the current art scene is too overly intellectual for him, and abstract pictures are not his thing. He wants to create works that are immediately "understandable" to any viewer and can therefore be distributed on a massive scale. His models are consumer goods and the media industry.

When he discovers the silkscreen technique in 1962 and realizes how easy and inexpensive it is in his initial trials, everything moves very quickly: Warhol, as he now calls himself, sets up his first studio in Manhattan, which he tellingly names "The Factory," and with the help of several assistants, he creates reproductions of soup cans, newspaper articles, and celebrities — most famously Marilyn Monroe. The pictures are a hit, the art scene takes to them enthusiastically, and Warhol becomes a star.

Warhol is not the only one turning to mass culture and surface aesthetics. Roy Lichtenstein, who has moved from England to New York, magnifies comic strips to gigantic sizes; Claes Oldenbourg recreates everyday objects as large, soft sculptures; and Jasper Johns paints pictures of the U.S. flag in bright, flat colors.

They all use templates from the everyday world, creating images from images that immediately appeal to viewers because they are familiar. No one needs to be afraid of this art; there is no prior knowledge necessary to decipher it. Fresh and easily accessible, this is truly popular art, or Pop Art for short.

But to speak of a democratization of art would be to wrongly interpret the approach of the pop artists: they are not trying to involve the viewers or make them part of the formation process, as Jackson Pollock or Mark Rothko intend to do with their abstract art, which Pop Art explicitly turns against. Rather, they aestheticize the mechanism of consumption, which in their opinion has become the hallmark of modern society: If the U.S. president and Liz Taylor drink the same Coca-Cola as the bum on the street corner, then this proves, according to Warhol, that mass production has created a fairer society.

Pop artists are heavily criticized for their literally superficial observation of the world — their contributions to the opening of the art scene and their aesthetic innovations, however, remain undisputed.

Andy Warhol in front of his double portrait of Marilyn Monroe, 1962.

mecca of the revolutionaries

Algeria secedes from France

The filthiest colonial war in Africa ends on March 19, 1962, with Algeria's proclamation of independence. The country, which has been occupied since 1830, was considered an "integral part" of France, which sent tens of thousands of French settlers to Algeria. The "Franco-Algerians" annexed the fertile lands, became the ruling class, and suppressed all resistance on the part of the local people, who were degraded to the status of dependent small farmers, with extreme harshness; Arabic was considered a "foreign language" in this country.

Around 1910, the Algerians founded the first nationalist parties. Demonstrations and acts of violence followed. On Victory Day in Europe, May 8, 1945, French authorities and settler vigilantes murdered about 45,000 Algerians in the massacre of Sétif as retaliation for whites killed in demonstrations. In 1954, Ahmed Ben Bella founded the National Liberation Front (FLN), which then started an armed liberation struggle in November of that year. War breaks out, with indescribable atrocities on all sides, and violent demonstrations and assassinations also spill over into the French motherland, where General de Gaulle is elected president in 1959. French intellectuals and students in particular condemn the colonial presence of their country in Algeria and organize solidarity committees in support of the struggle of the Arabs and the FLN; they will later become a driving force in the student protest movement.

But it is not time for that yet: In April 1961, an attempted coup by right-wing generals, who planned to seize power and overthrow de Gaulle, is defeated in Algiers. In October, the Paris police force shoots, slays, and drowns some 200 Algerians during a demonstration supporting the FLN in Paris, and the government covers it up.

De Gaulle finally responds and grants Algeria independence in the 1962 Treaty of Évi-an. The battle-hardened FLN establishes its autocracy as a socialist party in Algiers, and Ahmed Ben Bella becomes the first president and enjoys great sympathy around the world. He makes himself the spokesman for all African independence movements and gives freedom fighters and revolutionary groups from all over the world refuge and combat training in Algeria. Algiers becomes a "mecca for revolutionaries"; Che Guevara and Nelson Mandela visit several times.

On the domestic front, Bella conducts extensive land reforms and launches a dynamic education and training program for the Arab population but fails to master the shortage of skilled labor, unemployment, and housing shortages. Sustainable change therefore only begins after the 1965 coup (see page 100).

A jubilant crowd in the Kasbah of Algiers after the country becomes independent on March 18, 1962.

1962 YEMEN

modern times reach the land of arabian nights

The fall of the monarchy in North Yemen

Yemen had been divided since the 19th century: The British occupied the south, while the north had been dominated by Shia imams and then by kings for the last 900 years. North Yemen remained backward and plagued by famine.

King Muhammad finally tries to catch up with modernization after his accession to the throne in 1962, but it is too late: The Free Officers Movement storms the royal palace in Sana'a and declares the "Yemen Arab Republic," which is immediately recognized internationally because many believe that this will finally propel Yemen into the 20th century.

The first president General Abdullah al-Sallal, tries to modernize all areas of Yemeni life, following the example set by socialist Egypt. His administration improves the infrastructure of the cities and promotes transportation and weak industry, such as cement production. However, agricultural plans to intensify the export of coffee and cotton and to restrict the cultivation of the drug Kath are barely implemented by the conservative peasant population. Modernization only reaches the cities, while the rural and mountain population holds on to its traditional way of life.

The deposed King Muhammad flees to the mountain tribes in the north and starts a struggle for power with financial and military support from Saudi Arabia. Egyptian President Nasser, on the other hand, supports the new government in Sana'a with an expeditionary corps and tactical aircraft and declares: "Yemen is the catalyst for a socialist future of Arabia." He plans to make North Yemen a toehold from which to overthrow the traditionalist monarchies in Saudi Arabia and the Emirates.

The war against the mountain tribes ends in 1970, after a total of 200,000 casualties, with the exile of the former king. Nasser had already with-drawn his troops from Yemen in 1967, after his defeat in the war against Israel, and his protégé al-Sallal is overthrown. In the same year, South Yemen frees itself from British rule and builds a socialist "People's Republic" following the Soviet example. The Great Powers and all Arab states intervene in the subsequent conflicts and reunification negotiations between North and South Yemen. It is part of the tragedy of Yemen that all attempts at independent development since 1962 have been thwarted by the interventions of foreign powers, even up to the present day.

Yemeni fighters greet the Egyptian president Nasser in Sana'a in May 1964.

a world congress of the clergy

The Second Vatican Council

Pope John XXIII, elected in 1958 at the age of 77 as a "transitional Pope," surprises the Curia in 1959 by announcing a council to clarify the position of the Church in the modern world. He uses the term *Aggiornamento*, a "bringing up-to-date" of the Church. No other event in the recent history of the Catholic Church has been so strongly fueled by an atmosphere of change as the Second Vatican Council, which begins in October 1962.

A visually colorful gathering of almost 2,500 councilors from 133 countries assembles in the tiered nave of St. Peter's Basilica to discuss, confer, and eventually pass 16 groundbreaking documents over four sessions. The press and non-Catholic observers are constantly present.

It starts with a bang: The Roman Curia has prepared position papers in advance for the Council to vote on. Led by the old cardinals Liénart (Lille) and Frings (Cologne), the bishops from around the world protest in dramatic speeches, overturn the bills, and force the appointment of ten conciliar commissions, which work out new papers in open discussions.

Reforms are adopted in almost every area. The ecumenical dialogue with non-Christian religions is also greatly expanded. The liturgy is fundamentally reformed: Since then, mass has been held in local languages at a freestanding altar with the priest facing his congregation. The council commits to human rights and democracy, and finally, in the last session — after intense debate — to the recognition of religious freedom as well. The progressive councilors prevail on nearly every issue, and the young churches of Latin America and Africa gain international attention for the first time.

After John XXIII dies in June 1963, Cardinal Montini of Milan, a moderate progressive, succeeds him as Paul VI. He brings the council to a satisfactory conclusion in December 1965, but with more forceful intervention than his predecessor.

Inspired by the momentum of change, mainly Western European bishops' conferences adopt position papers over the following years, often going beyond the council's decisions and addressing previously untouched issues, such as human sexuality, celibacy, or the primacy of the pope. Even up to the present day, however, the "spirit of the council" has continued to be contested within the Church, especially since reinvigorated conservatives see the council's decisions as a trigger for the decline of the Church.

The largest convention ever held by high-ranking officials of the Catholic Church takes place in St. Peter's Basilica in 1962.

1962 USA

students for a democratic society

Agenda for a Generation

Students for a Democratic Society (SDS) was one of the most important protest groups in America in the 1960s. Its history from idealistic, intellectual beginnings to fragmentation into violent splinter groups as the decade closed, would mirror perfectly the changes and radicalization taking place in the entire society.

In 1962 two recent graduates of the University of Michigan, Robert Haber and Tom Hayden, published the Port Huron Statement. Entitled "Agenda for a Generation" it focused on the sense of alienation, apathy, fear and anger that had gripped America's youth:

"We are people of this generation... looking uncomfortably to the world we inherit."

"When we were kids the United States was the wealthiest and strongest country in the world; the only one with the atom bomb, the least scarred by modern war, an initiator of the United Nations . . . As we grew, however, our comfort was penetrated by events too troubling to dismiss. First, the fact of human degradation, symbolized by the Southern struggle against racial bigotry . . . Second, the . . . Cold War, symbolized by the presence of the Bomb, brought awareness that we . . . might die at any time."

The SDS grew slowly until the escalation of civil rights protests in the South and the Tet Offensive in Vietnam in January 1965 which proved to be a watershed moment. Public opinion shifted dramatically to strong opposition to the war. In April 1965 the SDS organized a march on Washington. which drew 25,000 people. Extensive television coverage brought the protestors' message into homes across the nation. In November 1965 the SDS organized a second protest which drew 100,000 people and left no doubt that President Johnson was tragically out of touch with the youth of the nation.

By the end of the decade the SDS had more than 100,000 members but it soon disintegrated into groups with varying agendas, the Weathermen being one. Formed by Bernardine Dohrn, Jim Mellen and Mark Rudd, among the most radical members of the SDS, the Weathermen openly advocated violence as a way to reform society.

In 1968 Hayden was an active protestor at the Democratic National Convention in Chicago. He was arrested and tried as one of the Chicago Seven and after a five-year legal battle was acquitted of all charges. In 1972 he visited the North Vietnam capital of Hanoi with his future wife Jane Fonda, a trip widely viewed as an act of treason. Nevertheless, Hayden went on to serve 18 years in the California State Legislature.

Protestors race through the Los Angeles Civic Center, in a demonstration against American involvement in the Vietnam war.

silent spring

The birth of enviromentalism

A plane rushes over a flock of sheep and sprays them with insecticides. What seems absurd today is simply an economic precaution in the 1960s. General environmental consciousness as we know it today, or even environmental protection measures, do not exist in the early 1960s. Everything is geared toward production, economic growth, and consumption, and this end justifies all means.

In Europe, the River Rhine is a typical example: pharmaceutical and chemical companies, especially the potash industry in Alsace, are dumping their untreated waste into the river, which has already been polluted with 30,000 tons of chloride per day along the German-Dutch border since the mid-1950s. In 1961, the waterworks can hardly treat the river water to make it safe for drinking, and the responsible German Federal Minister, Siegfried Balke, calls the Rhine "the largest sewer in Europe" in 1962. In June 1969, the Rhine becomes eutrophic, and a toxic wave washes down the river. Starting in Koblenz, tens of thousands of dead fish line the banks, and the population is warned not even to wash their hands in the river.

Especially in forestry, but also in domestic gardens, DDT and other insecticides are unscrupulously used against insect pests and extensively distributed by means of misters and spray planes. Orchards and pastures are also sprayed, leading to severe contamination of fruit and dairy products. Insecticides running into rivers cause fish to die.

This begins to change when the acclaimed American author Rachel Carson publishes her evocative, factually grounded work *Silent Spring* in 1962. Carson reveals the incalculable consequences of pesticides, advocates biological pest control, and outlines the poisoning of a food chain, at one end of which stand human beings. Three of the 17 chapters describe the effects of pesticides on human fertility, genomes, and embryos as well as their carcinogenic effects. Although the food industry rages against the book, it is widely accepted around the world. The U.S. and other countries form government commissions and DDT is banned in most Western industries in the early 1970s.

Silent Spring has aroused ecological awareness and indirectly launched environmental movements, making it one of the most influential books of the 20th century.

A plane sprays a flock of sheep with DDT in Oregon.

1962

1962

on the verge of a third world war

The superpower clash during the Cuban Missile Crisis

"However harsh and terrible the solution, there would be no other." On the night of October 28, 1962, Cuban Prime Minister Fidel Castro loses his nerve and calls on the Soviet Union to launch a nuclear strike against the U.S. The world is standing on the brink of an abyss. The escalating dispute between the two superpowers over the deployment of Soviet missiles in Cuba, the "backyard of the U.S.," threatens to get completely out of control.

Prior to this, the Soviet Premier Nikita Khrushchev has ignored the U.S. naval blockade, which began on October 24, and moved his naval units and aircraft toward Cuba. How can a catastrophe be prevented? Any action, no matter from which side, could trigger a disastrous chain reaction. Behind the scenes, the military chiefs of staff are continuously negotiating, and there are hardliners on both sides who want a war. Kennedy shows determination and also prudence. Just as in Moscow, even the most casual actions and statements of the other side are recorded in Washington and interpreted as signs during the crisis.

At noon on October 28, Khrushchev finally relents. He withdraws his fleet and orders the dismantling of Soviet missiles in Cuba. In turn, the U.S. later withdraws weapons from Turkey. The world exhales.

The Cold War has reached its climax. All parties agree that a situation like this must never happen again. The experience of this near-catastrophe proves to be a healing shock and paves the way for the first cautious attempts at détente between the superpowers. To ensure direct communication between the two opposing nuclear powers in the future and to prevent misunderstandings, a hotline, also known as the "red telephone," is established between the White House and the Kremlin in 1963. The idea of "peaceful coexistence" prevails on both sides, and from now on, the preservation of world peace becomes the top priority.

A U.S. Navy destroyer forces one of the Soviet freighters, loaded with Cuban missiles, off its course in October 1962.

the tupamaros uprising

The long road from guerrilla to president

Although Uruguay was formally ruled democratically after the Second World War — with two parties, the Blancos and the Colorados, alternating in government — major economic crises and high unemployment led to severe unrest and uprisings in Uruguayan cities from 1959 onward, especially in the capital, Montevideo.

In 1963, the Tupamaros movement forms out of labor circles as a "city guerrilla," named after the indigenous rebel Túpac Amaru II, who led an insurrection against the Spanish occupiers in the 18th century.

The communist Tupamaros initially want to ridicule government authorities with clever, disrespectful campaigns. However, they also rob banks and distribute the money among the poor. When the government takes action against them by way of emergency laws beginning in 1968, they radicalize. In addition to bomb attacks on urban facilities, they abduct domestic and foreign high-ranking or influential personalities, interrogate them in their "people's prisons," and make their statements accessible to the public. The abductees are then either released or murdered. When they kidnap the American CIA agent and "security adviser" Daniel Mitrione in 1970 and kill him after ten days in a "people's prison," the government begins a systematic military intervention against the Tupamaros.

Revolutionary groups also take up this concept of the city guerrilla. In 1969, the "Tupamaros West Berlin" and the "Tupamaros Munich" are founded in West Germany by the communards Dieter Kunzelmann (Berlin) and Fritz Teufel (Munich). Both groups maintain close connections with the Fatah liberation movement in Palestine and commit a series of attacks on police and judicial facilities as well as Jewish cultural institutions, in protest against Israel, between 1969 and 1971. The German Tupamaros disband in 1970–71, and some of their members go into the terrorist underground. The German RAF and the Italian Red Brigades adopt the concept of abductions and "people's prisons" from the Tupamaros, as in the famous cases of Hanns-Martin Schleyer (1977) and Aldo Moro (1978).

After long struggles with the state, the Tupamaros stand in election as a political party in Uruguay in 1985. Their leader, José Mujica, who spent 14 years in solitary confinement, becomes president from 2010 to 2015.

In protest against the U.S. participation in the Pan-American Conference in Punta del Este, Uruguay, the Tupamaros execute a bomb attack on the district administration office on April 13, 1967.

1963 IRAN

the white revolution

Shah Reza Pahlavi modernizes Iran

When Shah Mohammed Reza Pahlavi receives an overwhelming majority in favor of his six-point reform program, the "White Revolution," in a popular referendum and then finally enforces it, women are cheering in the cities: they are granted active and passive suffrage for the first time. His campaign for active literacy among the rural population, in which conscripts are trained as assistant teachers to instruct children and adults, wins just as much popular approval as profit-sharing between workers and employees in businesses and the nationalization of forests and pastures.

The redistribution of farmland from large landowners and the clergy to the peasants and the privatization of state-owned enterprises to compensate the landowners proves controversial. The land reform turns about two million landless farmers into property owners for the first time, but 65% of them receive less than 12 acres of land. More than a million farmers remain landless and migrate to the cities searching for jobs, leading to enormous growth in urban areas. As a consequence, agricultural production decreases.

The Shiite clergy protest against women's voting rights and their own displacement from public education, but above all against the land reform, which is taking away the clergy's source of income — namely, the cultivation or leasing of land. Landowners and merchants join their protest. After speeches made by the Shah's greatest critic, Ayatollah Khomeini, who accuses him of rejecting Islam and being a tool of the U.S. and Israel, protests take place in the big cities. The Shah orders his forces to fire into the assembled crowds. Khomeini is arrested and exiled in 1964.

The Shah expands his social and health care programs and takes increasingly harsh action against his critics. His infamous secret police torture or eliminate dissidents. On the other hand, he tries to win over the clergy with the construction of new mosques. Despite the economic boom generated by oil revenues, very few Iranians really profit from the reforms. Immense social differences remain.

The majority disapproves of the Shah's unconditional dependence on the U.S., his reference to the ancient Persian kings, in whose tradition he sees himself, his aim of transforming the country into a Western industrial nation, and the Western lifestyle of his family. Various forces rise up against his dictatorship, finally bringing down the Shah's regime by the end of 1978. After the Shah's flight, Ayatollah Khomeini celebrates his triumphant return to Iran in February 1979.

Iranian peasants hold ownership deeds to newly acquired lands in their arms.

1963

franco-german reconciliation

The first step towards European unification

It seems like a miracle to contemporaries: Only 17 years after the end of the devastating Second World War, French President Charles de Gaulle and German Chancellor Konrad Adenauer demonstrate their unity in Bonn. Together they want to promote the unification of Europe. On September 5, 1962, on his visit to the capital of the Federal Republic, de Gaulle praises the "great German people" in German and euphorically concludes his speech: "Long live Bonn! Long live Germany! Long live the Franco-German friendship!"

Since 1958, both heads of state have been trying to overcome the ancient "hereditary enmity" between the two countries and thus secure peace on the continent permanently. However, it is only after the former general de Gaulle has assured himself of the broad support of the Germans that he is ready to sign. On January 22, 1963, both parties solemnly sign the "Treaty on Franco-German

Cooperation" in the Élysée Palace in Paris, which is intended to institutionally ensure friendly relations.

In addition to regular consultations between the heads of state and government ministers on questions of foreign and defense policy, the intensification of student exchange programs is also agreed. This gives young people from both countries the chance to become closer and to overcome the former mistrust.

Yet shortly after the signing of the friendship treaty, a new controversy arises between France and Germany. De Gaulle intends the treaty as a counterweight to the dominant role of the U.S. in Europe. Meanwhile, U.S. President Kennedy considers this Franco-German cooperation as a challenge to his plans of a transatlantic alliance and expresses his disapproval of the treaty, which he refers to as an "unfriendly act." In order to maintain close diplomatic relations with the U.S., the West German parliament ratifies the

treaty in May 1963 with a preamble, emphasizing the importance of Western Europe's integration into NATO under U.S. leadership and accepting Great Britain into the European Economic Community (EEC). This addition undermines de Gaulle's aim of creating an independent Europe as third force alongside the U.S. and the USSR.

Despite these initial hurdles, Franco-German reconciliation is a milestone on the path to the integration of Western Europe. What Winston Churchill once framed as a vision of a "United States of Europe" in 1948 gradually takes shape from 1957 onward, with the founding of the EEC. To this day, Germany and France are the two core countries of the European Union, significantly promoting the project of European unification.

French President Charles de Gaulle welcomes German Chancellor Konrad Adenauer on the steps of the Élysée Palace in Paris.

1963

the assassination of john fitzgerald kennedy

There will never be another Camelot again.

President Kennedy was the fourth American President assassinated in office. He was killed on November 22 as his motorcade drove through Dallas, Texas, with the President seated in an open car. In light of the tragic events that would occur in the coming weeks and the high hopes for great things expected of Kennedy, his death was a shock from which the United States would never fully recover.

The impact of the Kennedy assassination on Americans was magnified by the extensive television coverage. For days all regular television programming was suspended and the assassination and its aftermath saturated the media and the minds of the public. No one could miss it, especially when just days later Lee Harvey Oswald, the accused murderer, was himself assassinated in front of television cameras.

Kennedy's death was seen as only the beginning of a decade of violence in a nation seemingly determined to tear itself apart. Civil rights activist Malcom X would be assassinated in 1965 and both Martin Luther King Jr., leader of peaceful protests for equality, and Robert F. Kennedy, the President's brother and candidate for the Democratic nomination for President, would be assassinated in 1968. The fallout of these tragedies served only to exacerbate the deep divisions and violence that had plagued America since the assassination of President Abraham Lincoln a century earlier.

President Kennedy had been willing to risk nuclear war with the Soviet Union over Cuba and he had sent 400 Special Service soldiers to Vietnam in 1961, beginning America's involvement in a land war in Asia. What might have been had he lived, however, was never spoken of openly. Time had stopped for Kennedy. His legacy would be a dream that would never be realized, a golden age that never was.

In an interview published in LIFE magazine shortly after her husband's death, Jacqueline Kennedy recalled the popular song Camelot about King Arthur and a glorious age of chivalry, which had been one of his favorites. She summed up the feeling of irredeemable loss of what might have been when she said: "There'll be great Presidents again ... but there'll never be another Camelot again."

Kennedy's funeral procession through Washington, D.C. was modeled on that of Abraham Lincoln, one of Kennedy's heroes about whom he'd said in a campaign speech: "Some may say that a Democratic candidate for the Presidency has no right to invoke the name of Lincoln. I disagree. Abraham Lincoln belongs to the ages, and he belongs to all Americans, regardless of their party," Like Lincoln, Kennedy now belonged to the ages.

President Kennedy waving at the crowds minutes before his assassination in Dallas, Texas.

socialism in the middle east

The Ba'ath Party transforms Iraq and Syria

In February 1963, the Ba'ath Party seizes power in Iraq for the first time in a military coup. In March of that year, a similar coup is also successful in Syria. In Iraq, however, the party is bogged down by internal power struggles, loses its control over the country in November, and has to wait until July 1968 to finally establish itself in a second coup. In Syria, party infighting and changing governments also lead to chaos over the following years, until Hafez al-Assad secures his rule with a renewed Ba'ath Party in 1970.

Founded in 1940, the Ba'ath Party (in Arabic, Ba'ath means reawakening or rebirth, namely of the Arab nation) sees itself as a revolutionary nationalist movement under the slogan "Unity, Freedom, Socialism." It takes up some of the principles of modern Western political thought. In contrast to Pan-Islamic movements that strive for the unification of all Muslims, the Ba'ath Party is based on Pan-Arabism — that is, the unification of all Arabs, regardless of their religion. In addition, it intends to promote the secularization of public life and is therefore particularly popular among the religious minorities — Shiites, Christians, Druzees, and Alawites.

In both countries, the Ba'ath Party nationalizes the banks as well as large segments of industry and foreign trade and forces industrialization and the modernization of the cities, also through the construction of prestige buildings. The advancement of the lower and middle classes, the equality of men and women, and educational training, especially in technology, are specifically promoted. A minimum wage and fixed working hours are officially determined, and national social services are established. Control over education and the judiciary is taken from the Islamic Shari'ah and comes under the sole authority of the state and the party. So the modernization of both countries takes place in many economic and socio-political areas, but at the same time, the clan dictatorship of presidents Assad and Hussein prevails, and human rights violations occur on a massive scale.

Syria and Iraq soon grow apart from each other: While Assad pursues a militarily enforced socialism, the nationalized oil industry provides Iraq with a huge economic boom starting in 1972, which benefits large sections of the population.

Obsessed with power, Saddam Hussein takes advantage of this boom and strengthens his army for wars with Iran and Kuwait. After his fall in 2003, the U.S. occupiers dissolve the Ba'ath Party in Iraq, although it is still in power in Syria as the Neo-Ba'ath Party, with Bashar al-Assad as its leader.

Supporters of the Ba'ath Party in front of the airport in Damascus on March 31, 1963.

1963

fighting fallout

Nuclear test pollution and banning

After the Second World War, the victorious powers fiercely compete to possess of the most powerful and largest number of nuclear bombs. In the 1950s, nuclear weapons were repeatedly tested — hundreds of times in remote areas, in the vast deserts of Nevada and on the steppes of Kazakhstan, on remote Pacific atolls or in the depths of the ocean. Regular bomb tests serve the USA, the Soviet Union, the United Kingdom, and France as mutual deterrence and are supposed to provide research data. In 1962 alone, during the first climax of the Cold War, over 180 nuclear weapons are tested around the world.

The tests cause an alarming increase in radioactivity in the earth's atmosphere. This provokes worldwide protests and resolutions — with extraordinary success: on August 5, 1963, exactly 18 years after the first atomic bomb was dropped on Hiroshima, delegations from the U.S., the Soviet Union, and Great Britain come together in the Kremlin to sign an agreement banning nuclear weapon tests in the atmosphere, in space, and underwater. Underground tests continue to be allowed. The moratorium on nuclear testing establishes legal control mechanisms for the first time, and these become the precursors for later arms control agreements.

The signing of the Partial Nuclear Test Ban Treaty raises great hopes. British Prime Minister Sir Alec Douglas-Home promises that "each family will from now on be free of fear that their unborn children will be affected by artificially created poison in the atmosphere." And UN Secretary-General U Thant even states that the danger of an impending nuclear war is dispelled by the treaty.

The concentration of pollutants in the air indeed decreases rapidly, but the nuclear arms race continues unabated for years. The number of nuclear powers even increases with the addition of China, India, Pakistan, and finally Israel and North Korea.

In the Treaty on the Non-Proliferation of Nuclear Weapons in 1968, the nuclear powers agree to the common goal of complete nuclear disarmament for the first time.

Surface detonation of a nuclear test bomb in the Nevada desert.

1963

the march on washington

A milestone in the Civil Rights Movement

August 28, 1963 is a splendid summer day in Washington. Supported by church, labor, and civil rights organizations, demonstrators from all over the country are pouring into the government district to advocate for the civil rights of African-Americans and the abolition of racial segregation in the Southern states.

An estimated 250,000 people listen as Martin Luther King Jr. begins his speech on the steps leading up to the Lincoln Memorial. The prominent civil rights activist is nervous, deviates from his manuscript, and improvises his vision in a free speech: "I have a dream that my four little children will one day live in a nation where they will not be judged by the color of their skin, but by the content of their character." Emphatically, the Baptist minister finishes his speech with an appeal to freedom: "When we allow freedom to ring — when we let it ring from every village and every hamlet, from every state and every

city, we will be able to speed up that day when all of God's children [...] will be able to join hands and sing in the words of the old Negro spiritual: 'Free at last! Free at last! Thank God Almighty, we are free at last!'"

One year later, King receives the Nobel Peace Prize and is already regarded as the central embodiment of the non-violent civil rights movement. This is also because the mass demonstration actually ends peacefully. U.S. President Kennedy is impressed and reaffirms his intentions to pass civil rights legislation.

However, the black liberation movement remains divided. The radical activist Malcolm X (see page 74) criticizes the demonstration as a deal with the "white devil." And indeed, it will be a white racist who assassinates Martin Luther King Jr. on April 4, 1968 (see page 152).

Martin Luther King Jr. in Washington, D.C. on August 28, 1963.

1963

mr. tambourine man

Bob Dylan becomes the involuntary icon of the protest generation

A rusty voice singing profound poetic lyrics to strange guitar music: John Hammond, an experienced manager at the large record label Columbia, has never encountered anything like this. But he likes what he hears, and so he takes a certain Robert Allen Zimmermann, who calls himself Bob Dylan, under contract at Columbia Records in 1962 as the first folk singer.

His debut album, "Bob Dylan," remains an insider's tip inside the scene. Dylan mainly owes his meteoric rise over the next few years to his longtime lover, the folk singer Joan Baez. She had become famous in the late 1950s through her protest songs against racial discrimination and military interventions. Her version of the anti-war song "Where Have All the Flowers Gone" has turned into a protest anthem around the world.

Dylan quickly becomes famous in the summer of 1963 thanks to a joint U.S. tour with Baez. The sound and lyrics of songs like "Blowin' in the Wind" appeal to the audience because they describe the changed worldview of a young generation. With "The Times They Are a-Changin'" in 1964, Dylan writes the programmatic song of his time. He becomes a star and everyone — not just his fans — listens.

Although Dylan refuses to be portrayed as the voice of his generation, his songs are sung during demonstrations and interpreted by many as a musical articulation of their demands. However, the more his fans want to monopolize him, the more Dylan withdraws from the public eye.

Pop music reaches a new political dimension in the 1960s in the music of Bob Dylan and Joan Baez, but also through the work of other folk musicians, like Woody Guthrie, Phil Ochs, and Pete Seeger: popular music is no longer just entertainment; it also carries current social and political messages. This makes it a serious art form. In recognition of the profound impact of Dylan's music, and his lyrics in particular, he is finally awarded the Nobel Prize in Literature in 2016.

Joan Baez and Bob Dylan perform together at the March on Washington (see page 62).

"yeah, yeah, yeah"

The Beatles change the world of pop

In Great Britain, they are *the* cultural sensation of 1963. Wherever they go, traffic collapses and female fans scream and faint. In Birmingham, John Lennon, Paul McCartney, Ringo Starr, and George Harrison even have to dress up as police officers to be able to leave the stage.

The music world has never seen anything like the Beatles. Everything the "Fab Four" put on the market sells by the millions. Songs with catchy beats and banal, harmless lyrics like "She Loves You" and "I Want to Hold Your Hand" storm the charts.

The following year, "Beatlemania" reaches new dimensions: on March 31, 1964, the Beatles become the only act ever to occupy the first five positions on the U.S. billboard charts. Nearly 40% of the U.S. population watch the Beatles' first appearance on U.S. television in February 1964. On their first world tour, the band fills entire football stadiums.

The long-haired Beatles are a pop-cultural model as well as the icons of a rebellious young generation. Both the loud rock music with its driving beat and the outer appearance of the musicians provoke conservative society. Their "feminine" mop-top hair-cuts mock their formal "male" suit-and-tie outfits. Many people perceive the often quite cheeky behavior of the Liverpool boys in public as impertinent. The concerns of the British establishment in 1964 are so severe that Beatlemania sparks a heated debate in the British House of Commons on the moral conduct of British youth. Conservatives brand Beatles fans as "the dull, the idle, the failures" of their generation.

Policemen desperately try to push back a crowd of Beatles fans in front of Buckingham Palace.

1963

1963 SWEDEN

a sex scandal at the movies

Ingmar Bergman's permissive film The Silence

September 23, 1963. The first Swedish cinema audience watches the new Ingmar Bergman film *The Silence* and is shocked: a woman masturbating, a woman watching a couple having sex, a woman having quick sex with a stranger, and a child having body contact with its naked mother. The cultural world is greatly excited. Church authorities cry "Scandal!" Outraged citizens take the matter to court to enforce a ban. The Swedish parliament holds a heated debate on censorship. The result: Hundreds of thousands of Swedes crowd into cinemas so as not to miss this "godless" film.

The reactions are similar in other European countries, although only a few screen the original uncensored version. In the United States, cinemas show a shortened version, and in France the film is initially prohibited.

Particularly violent protests occur in West Germany, where the uncensored film is restricted to viewers over 18 years old.

When attempts to legally oppose this "obscene" film fail, conservative politicians found the initiative "Aktion Saubere Leinwand" (Campaign for a Clean Screen), which publicly calls for legal measures against such "immoral and questionable works."

Despite all this, many film critics are convinced of the artistic value of this drama about two sisters from the very beginning: Rarely has people's loneliness in a modern, "godless" world been depicted more penetratingly on screen.

In the end, this great fuss primarily helps the film break records at box offices across Europe. Conservative moralists keep to themselves, while cineasts around the world celebrate the film, though often on the quiet. On the one hand, Bergman breaks sexual taboos on screen with his "shock film," thus paving the way for the sexual revolution, but on the other hand, he also opens the door to less qualified imitators, who readily follow with lots of sleazy scandal films.

Causing an outrage in the 1960s: A boy washes his naked mother's back.

1963 WEST GERMANY

the first auschwitz trial

Confrontation with the Nazi past as incentive for the student movement

The prevailing, fundamental agreement on a collective silence about the Nazi past gradually breaks down in West Germany toward the end of the 1950s. First, the Ulm Einsatzkommando trial in 1958 forces the administration, which is still infused with Nazi lawyers, to cooperate with the newly established Central Office of the State Justice Administrations for the Investigation of National Socialist Crimes in Ludwigsburg.

Prepared by the Hessian state attorney general Fritz Bauer and involving 20 defendants, the first Frankfurt Auschwitz trial takes place between December 1963 and August 1965, and is followed by others. The defendants are not high officials, but direct perpetrators and henchmen of the Nazi extermination apparatus. The emotional statements made by 360 Auschwitz survivors shock the press and the public, as does the described brutality of the perpetrators, who have established new existences as ordinary citizens after the war

and show no sense of guilt. Auschwitz becomes a synonym for the horrors of the Holocaust.

The court has to handle enormous piles of documents, especially since it rejects the assistance Poland offers, for reasons of the Cold War. It is indeed a small sensation when members of the court visit Auschwitz, the former concentration camp, for a site inspection at the end of 1964.

After 183 days of proceedings, the verdicts are issued: six life sentences, eleven shorter prison sentences, and three acquittals.

In addition to the Auschwitz trial, further court cases are brought against the personnel of the extermination camps in Chelmno/Kulmhof, Belzec, Sobibor, and Treblinka between 1963 and 1966, revealing profound horrors and atrocities and charging the defendants, who have also set up a façade of harmless civility, with complicity in murder in at least 360,000 cases.

During this entire period, and since the beginning of

the Eichmann trial (see page 30), press articles, eyewitness reports, and specialist books finally provide detailed background information about the perfidious system of the Nazi concentration and extermination camps. Most notably, this promotes long-avoided discussions between the generations. Young people ask their parents, professors, and colleagues: "What did you do and know?" And they criticize the hypocritical double standards of their parents' generation. The reprocessing of the Nazi past becomes an important driving force in the West German student protests and continues to be a force for change to this day.

One year after the beginning of the Auschwitz trial, members of the court and journalists inspect the former concentration camp on December 14, 1964.

nelson mandela

The struggle against apartheid in South Africa

When Nelson Mandela rises to speak on April 20, 1964, the courtroom goes dead quiet. For years, the South African political activist has been fiercely fighting the racist apartheid system, and now he is on trial for the alleged planning of armed sabotage. As always, he is very well dressed, purposely distinguishing himself from common street fighters.

In a quiet and confident manner, Mandela gives a four-hour speech on the humiliating situation of black people in South Africa. Facing a possible death sentence, Mandela calls for a true democracy and equal political rights for all, black and white, in an emphatic closing address. "During my lifetime I have fought against white domination, and I have fought against black domination. I have cherished the ideal of a democratic and free society in which all persons live together in harmony and with equal opportunities. It is an ideal which I hope to live for and to achieve. But, if it needs be, it is an ideal for which I am prepared to die."

Mandela's moving words help him — he is not sentenced to death, but to life imprisonment for sabotage and armed struggle. Furthermore, the speech continues to have an effect because it impresses parts of the critical public in South Africa and receives a great response in the international press. Ever since, the worldwide anti-apartheid movement has been closely linked to Mandela's fate. Solidarity committees advocating for the end of apartheid in South Africa and for Mandela's release gradually take shape.

Over the following years, the South African government will repeatedly offer to release him if his party, the ANC, renounces its armed struggle against apartheid. Yet Mandela always refuses, and he is only released from prison after 27 years, on February 11, 1990, by order of President F.W. de Klerk. On May 9, 1994, he is elected the first black president of South Africa.

Nelson Mandela during a break at his trial.

malcolm x and muhammad ali

Two fighters for African-American liberation

Malcolm Little, who rejects the surnames of blacks in the U.S. as a legacy of slavery and therefore calls himself Malcolm X, is the radical black opponent of Martin Luther King Jr., whom he denounces as a "house negro" of the whites. While the latter campaigns for nonviolence and reconciliation (see page 62), Malcolm X, a preacher for the radical Black Muslims ("Nation of Islam"), fights for an autonomous black state that would have to be established even against the will of the whites if necessary. "White supremacy" is to be resisted by any means necessary.

When the Olympic boxing champion Cassius Clay meets Malcolm X in 1964, his worldview fundamentally changes. The establishment is horrified when Clay, who up to this point has been especially infamous for his loud-mouthed boasts ("I am the greatest"), discloses that he has joined the Black Muslim movement after winning the World Heavyweight Championship in 1964. He discards his "slave name" and calls himself Muhammad Ali from then on. When the extremely popular, self-appointed "King of the World" refuses to be drafted to fight in Vietnam in 1966, with his famous statement: "Man, I ain't got no quarrel with them Viet Cong, no Viet Cong ever called me nigger," he loses his world title and his boxing license.

By this time, Malcolm X is no longer alive. Their friendship began to unravel when Malcolm X increasingly turned away from the idea of black separatism and toward moderate Sunni Islam. On February 21, 1965, the alleged traitor is shot in New York, presumably by members of the Nation of Islam.

Later, Muhammad Ali also decides to adhere to moderate Islam, but he remains loyal to the fight for the "black cause." For Ali, entering the ring to fight the unbeaten boxing champion George Foreman in Kinshasa in 1974, the fight is mainly about "racial problems, Vietnam. All of that." After he sensationally wins the "Rumble in the Jungle" and recaptures his world title, the whole world — black and white — celebrates Muhammad Ali as the greatest boxer of all time.

Two headstrong personalities briefly fight together for the African-American cause: Muhammad Ali and Malcolm X, 1964.

fighting against a one-dimensional society

Herbert Marcuse's influence on the student movement

The student movement of the 1960s has many intellectual fathers among the philosophers and sociologists critical of capitalism. Herbert Marcuse plays a special role because he is more radical in his demands and because, as a German-American writer, he can provide the U.S. as well as the Western European student protests with a theoretical foundation.

Having emigrated from Germany to the United States in 1933, the Jewish thinker works closely with Max Horkheimer and Theodor W. Adorno, who return to Germany after the war, inspiring German students as the heads of the Frankfurt School of critical theory. Marcuse stays in the U.S., holding university chairs in Massachusetts and California, but also at the Free University of Berlin.

His two major works become extremely influential in the search for a "revolutionarily renewed society." In *Eros and Civilization* (1955), he combines the thinking of Marx and Sigmund Freud. He sees Freud's pleasure principle, and hence the imagination, as ruled by the reality principle, which degenerates into performance pressure, alienation, instinct suppression, and destructiveness under capitalism. In contrast, a free Marxist society works toward putting an end to the self-oppression of human beings, turning the pleasure principle into the reality principle and utilizing the forces hitherto used to exploit human beings and destroy nature for the creation of art and culture. The emerging sexual revolution owes a lot to Marcuse's work.

His second major work *One-Dimensional Man* (1964), has the greatest impact. It criticizes the "one-dimensional," affirmative attitude of the public and of science in modern societies that avoids ethical and political judgments and seeks refuge in apparently neutral technological and scientific progress. Exploitive relationships and nuclear weapons are not called into question. Against this affirmative thinking, which serves the status quo, Marcuse sets up the "great refusal," which involves negation through criticism and the denial of mere continuation. While many students interpret the "Great Refusal" as an exit, Marcuse is concerned with a rational criticism that interprets human beings as multidimensional and points out alternatives to the existing order, thereby at least projecting the utopia of a self-liberating society. However, according to Marcuse, many institutions that currently exist in society must be "negated" or radically changed.

The philosopher Herbert Marcuse at a panel discussion.

the mods and swinging london

A different kind of youth movement

Motor scooters — pimped with scores of mirrors — and parkas are their trademark. The modernists, or mods as they call themselves, are a youth movement in Swinging London during the 1960s. Their territory stretches from Wembley to the West End, where they form a strong countercultural scene aimed at one thing in particular: being non-conformist and different from their working-class or lower middle-class parents.

This starts with their clothing style, which stands out from ordinary mass-market fashion. Hidden underneath green parkas, the mods wear smart, tailor-made suits with matching neckties, often combined with designer shoes. Expensive rather than cheap, conspicuous instead of adapted. Their style of dress corresponds exactly with London's fashionable avant-garde, which combines color and originality with elegance (see page 34).

The mods' professed goal is to show up at work even after nightly excesses. And the nights are always long: Doped with uppers, especially amphetamines, the mods dance to soul, ska, and British beat music for hours, thereby setting their own trend.

The wild rock group The Who, founded around Pete Townshend in 1964, is one of the most influential English beat bands to emerge from among the ranks of the mods. Their song "My Generation," with its famous line: "I hope I die before I get old," becomes a hymn for British youth.

On Easter weekend 1964, mods and youths of the rocker movement engage in extensive fist and chair fights in the English seaside resort of Brighton. The dramatic war headlines and TV reports on these events make the mods known to a wide audience. They find many imitators on the continent, and strong mod movements also develop in Germany and France.

The rivalry between mods and rockers will also be the subject of the concept album *Quadrophenia* (1973) by The Who and will be immortalized in 1979 in the motion picture of the same name.

Young mod John Rogers with a scooter that boasts 27 lamps, plus horns, mirrors, badges, and chrome mascots.

the great society

The Great Society rests on abundance and liberty for all.

Lyndon Baines Johnson was one of the most powerful Democrats in Congress with a reputation for getting things done. His selection as vice-president to run with Kennedy in 1960 was intended to win over the conservative Southern wing of the party, never comfortable with Kennedy's stance on civil rights or the expansion of federal over state powers.

Social Security had been the only nationwide social program in America with the individual states retaining control of education, health and welfare programs as they saw fit and could afford. But Johnson had a different vision for America.

After his election in 1964, Johnson was determined not only to carry out Kennedy's plans for social change but to launch his own vision of a more just and inclusive America. In May 1964 in a speech at the University of Michigan, where Kennedy had launched the Peace Corps, Johnson unveiled his plans for the Great Society, the most ambitious and contro-versial package of social legislation since the 1930s.

"The Great Society... demands an end to poverty and racial injustice, to which we are totally committed in our time. But that is just the beginning. The Great Society is a place where every child can find knowledge to enrich his mind and to enlarge his talents. It is a place where leisure is a welcome chance to build and reflect, not a feared cause of boredom and restlessness. It is a place where the city of man serves not only the needs of the body and the demands of commerce but the desire for beauty and the hunger for community."

The key planks of the Great Society included: the War on Poverty, programs to improve living conditions and welfare entitlements; sixty separate bills on education to provide teacher training, better-equipped classrooms, minority scholarships and low-interest student loans; Medicare and Medicaid to provide health care to Americans over sixty-five; legislation to promote clean air and water; the National Endowment for the Arts and Humanities to support artists, performers and writers; the Voting Rights Act to remove racially motivated restrictions on voting; the Job Corps to provide training for young men and women who would otherwise be unable to find suitable employment; and a special Head Start program to address the needs of pre-school age children from disadvantaged families.

The Great Society effectively removed sole control of health, education, welfare and broad social policy from individual states, introduced uniform standards countrywide and centered the administration of social programs in the bureaucracy of the federal government.

Lyndon B. Johnson talks with civil rights leaders James Farmer, Martin Luther King Jr. and Whitney Young, in the White House.

lsd and the acid test

An attempt to change the world by expanding the mind

"I sank into a not unpleasant intoxicated[-]like condition [...] In a dreamlike state, with eyes closed (I found the daylight to be unpleasantly glaring), I perceived an uninterrupted stream of fantastic pictures, extraordinary shapes with intense, kaleidoscopic play of colors. After some two hours this condition faded away."

This is how the Swiss chemist Albert Hoffmann describes his intoxication experience after discovering LSD by accident while conducting experiments in 1943. The CIA is soon interested in the hallucinogen — but it remains unknown to the public until the beginning of the 1960s, when a group of freaks propagates LSD as a consciousness-expanding drug for the self-liberation of humankind. The Boston psychologist Timothy Leary and the famous Californian author Ken Kesey (*One Flew Over the Cuckoo's Nest*) are among the most prominent consumers, using psychedelic drugs such as LSD, also known as acid, to expand their consciousness and perception in order to discover a new approach to the inner self. This imaginary escape from the real world is supposed to help one redesign the world afterwards.

In the summer of 1964, Kesey and his friends buy an old school bus in San Francisco, paint it in bright, day-glo colors, turn up the music, and go on an LSD propaganda tour across the U.S. as the "Merry Pranksters" — destination: New York. This is the beginning of an LSD hysteria throughout the country and the birth of the "hippie movement." The Pranksters produce posters and flyers inviting people to Acid Tests ("Can you pass the LSD test?"). In this way, they keep changing events into LSD experiences always surrounded by psychedelic music and people dancing in a trance.

However, as a result of mass consumption, the dangers of an LSD trip are also becoming more and more apparent: people are jumping out of windows or injuring themselves or others. In 1966, LSD is banned in the U.S., but this makes little difference to the consumption rates at first. With the gradual fading of the hippie movement by the end of the 1960s, LSD loses its importance and is replaced by even harsher drugs.

A dancer high on LSD at an Acid Test party in San Francisco.

1964

flower power in the far east

Asia's most famous girl band Dara Puspita

They are a real provocation to the traditional society of Indonesia. Not only does the band consist exclusively of women — so far, women in Indonesia have performed as back-up singers or in traditional folklore groups, if at all. Moreover, these young musicians present themselves in miniskirts and proclaim Western, liberal, emancipatory values.

Founded in 1964 around lead guitarist Titiek Adji Rachman, the band Dara Puspita ("Flower Girl") breaks with Indonesian customs both musically and culturally — and it achieves remarkable success. With its psychedelic rock sound, which combines Indonesian musical traditions with Western pop music, the first girl group fascinates audiences not only in Indonesia, but also in neighboring countries such as Thailand and Malaysia. Suddenly there is a whole new youth scene everywhere that wants to break out of traditional social conventions. Music connects this generation around the world and strengthens their desire for change.

Sukarno, the left-wing nationalist ruler of the Republic of Indonesia, which became independent in 1945, is less enthusiastic. He condemns Western music as a "form of mental disease," which increasingly puts the band under public pressure. Another pop group, the Koes Brothers, who encouraged Dara Puspita in their early days, are arrested in 1965 for performing covers of Beatles songs.

At first, the girl band continues to perform in Bangkok, then they leave the country in 1968 to go on a European tour for several years. In the meantime, Indonesia changes from an authoritarian republic to a brutal military dictatorship. General Suharto is officially declared President of Indonesia in 1967 and will rule the country as a dictator until 1998.

Dara Puspita returns home in late 1971, but they break up shortly afterward, in 1972 — apparently for quite traditional reasons: the girls want to marry and start families.

A Dara Puspita album cover from the early 1970s.

revolution from above

The brief flowering of democracy in Afghanistan

Afghanistan is a country traditionally dominated by tribes, and the central government has difficulties asserting itself. Since the 19th century, it has been a pawn in the game between the rival superpowers Russia and Great Britain, with Britain having the upper hand. A first attempt at modernization and independence by King Amanullah, who opened the country to European economic intervention, ended in 1929 with his overthrow by the Islamists.

When the last king, Mohammed Zahir Shah, ascends to the throne in 1933, the country initially still stands under the conservative rule of his uncles, but when he starts to govern on his own in 1963, he sees the necessity for an extensive modernization of all areas of society. In 1964, he convenes the Grand Council of tribal chiefs to secure their approval of his reform program. In the same year, he issues a constitution, turning Afghanistan into a constitutional monarchy. This opens the country to foreign economic investment and promotes intense cultural exchange, particularly with the countries of Europe and with the U.S. During these years, Kabul and other cities present a colorful array of Afghans in both traditional and modern dress, and even the first miniskirts are spotted.

With the help of foreign aid, roads, airports, and factories are built, and electricity and telecommunication networks are expanded. Especially among students in the cities, intellectual freedom blossoms, finding its expression in parades and discussion circles. Girls are allowed to attend public schools for the first time, and women are given the right to vote. After the first free elections in September 1965, the king appoints Kubra Noorzai as Minister of Public Health, thereby appointing the first woman to an Afghan cabinet.

But democratization and modernization are not just a matter of approval. In rural regions, the archaic social system can hardly be changed.

Party contests and famines in the provinces ultimately lead to a coup, led by Mohammed Daoud Khan, the king's cousin and former prime minister, in July 1973 and to the abolishment of the monarchy, ending the "good years" of freedom for Afghans. Daoud Khan's brutal military dictatorship, his assassination by the army in 1978, and the takeover by the Communists, who call Soviet troops into the country at the end of 1979, plunge Afghanistan into a long and bloody civil war, the consequences of which continue to have an effect even today.

Tradition meets modernity: A governor in Western clothing meets with a village council in his district in 1967.

"man is condemned to be free"

Jean-Paul Sartre and Existentialism

It is *the* scandal of the season: On October 22, 1964, the Swedish Academy announces that the Nobel Prize in Literature has been awarded to the French writer Jean-Paul Sartre — and Sartre immediately declines! He does not want to be corrupted by the prize. The French tabloids clamor, and the cultural scene is outraged.

And yet, the decision seems logical for a thinker who is known for his independence and his sense of freedom — the very ideas for which he is supposed to be honored.

At the time, Sartre is not only regarded as one of the most influential intellectuals in France; his dramatic and philosophical writings are eagerly received all over the Western world. Sartre's major philosophical work *Being and Nothingness* is published as early as 1943, making him the founder of existentialism, which primarily flourishes after the war. In his view, the individual human is confronted with a desperate freedom apart from the collective. There is no God, no being, no human destiny; man is what he makes of himself. As much as he tries to disguise this with self-deception and insincerity, he remains "condemned to be free."

Existentialism becomes the guiding principle and way of life for a whole circle of serious-minded, black-clad intellectuals, artists, and contemporary followers, and the actively committed Sartre is their prophet. The increasingly blind thinker is a moral authority, intervenes in political discussions with his radical positions, and organizes protest actions, for example against the Vietnam War. Responding to demands for his imprisonment, President de Gaulle, certainly no friend to Sartre, answers: "You don't arrest Voltaire."

More and more, Sartre turns toward non-party Marxism, as his second philosophical masterpiece, *Critique of Dialectical Reason* (1960), already indicates.

He is a passionate supporter of the student revolution, although he does not become their leading theorist: neo-Marxists, structuralists, and the critical theory of the Frankfurt School have surpassed him. Until the very end, however, he intervenes, criticizes, and lectures with a steady rhetorical brilliance, even though some of his ideas may also overshoot the mark. He is admired and forgiven for his vanities and his lusting after young women. Completely blind, he dies in Paris in April 1980; 50,000 people attend the funeral procession and throw flowers onto his coffin.

Jean-Paul Sartre at his desk around 1964.

1964

the beginning of the u.s. intervention in vietnam

A war leading to worldwide protests

No other war after 1945 has penetrated the consciousness of the world public so profoundly and led so many to ongoing protests and such a sustained rethinking as the Vietnam War. For the war-stricken people of Vietnam, this war is yet another gruesome stage in their bloody post-colonial history.

After the expulsion of the French colonial rulers during the First Indochina War (1945–54), the country is divided: the north is governed by the Communist Vietminh of Ho Chi Minh, supported by the Soviet Union and China, while the U.S.-supported Catholic dictator Ngo Dinh Diem rules the south. His unscrupulous resettlement policy, corrupt family reign, and struggle against former allies (both sects and paramilitaries) lead to a civil war, in which the north also gets involved by sending communist fighters down the "Ho Chi Minh Trail" to support the rebels in the south.

Together with some Communists from the north, southern opposition groups form the "National Front for the Liberation of South Vietnam," also known as the "Viet Cong," which is quickly joined by poor peasants and controls 75% of the rural areas of South Vietnam by the end of 1961. In the same year, the U.S. secretly stations small, heavily armed military units in South Vietnam. As Diem uses the situation to suppress the peasants and eventually also the Buddhists, President Kennedy withdraws his military advisors. On November 2, 1963, dissatisfied officers murder Diem and his clan. On November 22, Kennedy is assassinated.

The new U.S. President, Lyndon B. Johnson, wants to harden his stance against the Communists and installs governments in South Vietnam that reject any form of rapprochement with the North. In order to win over the U.S. public and convince Congress of the necessity of direct participation in the war, he stages the "Gulf of Tonkin Incident" in August 1964: A U.S. warship sinks a North Vietnamese torpedo boat in the Gulf of Tonkin off the coast of North Vietnam, claiming that the torpedo boat had attacked first. The U.S. air raids that immediately bomb Hanoi as "retaliation" have long been prepared. In this way, Johnson overcomes all hurdles, receives the approval of Congress, and wins the elections in a landslide in November.

With over half a million soldiers stationed in Vietnam at the height of the war in 1969, the U.S. is involved in a military conflict that will also turn into a nightmare, spiralling out of control. The war, however, will also provoke worldwide anti-war and protest movements of unprecedented dimensions.

The first U.S. Marine regiments are deployed to South Vietnam in the fall of 1964.

free speech at berkeley

The birth of the international student movement

The revolution comes in socks. Philosophy student Mario Savio takes his shoes off before he climbs on top of the police car to talk to his fellow students — after all, the protest is supposed to be absolutely peaceful. For hours, students have been holding a sit-in to prevent the departure of the car, in which their fellow student Jack Weinberg is being held. "We are human beings," Savio emphatically cries out to his comrades. "There is a time when the operation of the machine becomes so odious, makes you so sick at heart, that you can't take part […] and you've got to make it stop!" By machines Savio means not only the police car, but also the "machine-like," inhumane administrative and educational system of the university as well as the police. After a 32-hour blockade, the students come to an agreement with the university management: Weinberg is not arrested for agitation on campus and the first relaxing of campus regulations is achieved.

Since 1960, especially in liberal California, leftist student groups have been fighting for more direct democracy, better social service providers, and equal opportunities in life. However, they are not allowed to advocate these demands on university campuses, because political activities and demonstrations of any kind are generally prohibited on campus. Savio and his comrades, including many women, want to change this. The university should not be reduced to a production workshop preserving the status quo, but should become the motor of social change. At first the university management remains rigid, but after a teaching strike involving nearly half of the university staff in December 1964, it fully relents. Politics now also become a legal part of the university landscape, and students are finally recognized as a political factor that can no longer be ignored.

The Berkeley slogan "Don't trust anyone over 30" is not the only thing that becomes famous around the world. Above all, the protests have a long-standing influence due to their initiation of new forms of non-violent resistance: sit down strikes (sit-ins) and university discussions about politics (teach-ins) become central forms of academic protest in Europe over the following years.

From the roof of a police car, Mario Savio speaks to his fellow students on the campus of the University of California at Berkeley on October 1, 1964.

1964

hare krishna

Indian teachings reach the West

Starting in the 1960s, groups of young people turn up in American and European cities chanting mantras and wearing long Indian robes, often with shaved heads. They are disciples of the Hare Krishna movement, or more specifically, the International Society for Krishna Consciousness (ISKCON), founded in 1966.

The founder, Hindu scholar A.C. Bhaktivedanta Swami Prabhupaba, travels to the United States with his writings in 1965 and encounters young dropouts, hippies, and politically frustrated people in California who recognize him as their teacher. From his own translation of the main Hindu scripture, the Bhagavad Gita, he derives his teachings, which are deeply rooted in Indian philosophy. According to his teachings, Krishna, an avatar (manifestation) of the god Vishnu, is considered a perfect manifestation of the divine, whose invocation in the mantra of the individual soul of the disciple enables a "devotional service" through meditation with the aim of (re)awakening the love of God.

Popularized by the musical *Hair* and songs by George Harrison and others, the famous mantra of the invocation is:

"Hare Krishna, Hare Krishna, Krishna Krishna, Hare Hare, Hare Rama, Hare Rama, Rama Rama, Hare, Hare."

"Hare" stands for the divine energy, embodied by Krishna's companion Radha, and "Rama" means joy, which is also an avatar of the god Vishnu. Community members are required to chant this mantra daily in 16 cycles with 108 repetitions. Indian musical instruments, such as harmoniums, cymbals, and double-sided drums, usually accompany the chanting.

The Hare Krishna disciples engage in active but nonaggressive missionary work in the inner cities by distributing books and writings, which they conceive of as a form of "worship," but which is also criticized in some countries. Since some disciples temporarily break away from their families and environments, the movement is classified not only as a new religion, but also as a youth cult.

Socio-critical escapists are inspired by the Hare Krishnas' complete departure from traditional Western beliefs and opening up toward Indian Eastern thinking as well as meditation. The monotonous repetition of the mantra frequently puts the disciples in a trance-like, psychedelic state that critics regard as autosuggestion. The movement is respected for its radical pacifism, which understands all living things as parts of the divine, and for its abstinence from meat consumption, alcohol, and intoxicants as well as gambling and speculative trading.

Members of the Hare Krishna movement in Central Park in New York.

the bad boys from england

The Rolling Stones are unstoppable

"Daaa-daaa-da-da-daaa...": According to legend, the "five notes that shook the world" (Newsweek) come to Rolling Stones guitarist Keith Richards in a dream. Still halfway asleep, he reaches for his guitar, pushes the record button on his cassette recorder, and creates a riff that will be blasting on every radio station a few weeks later. In the morning, he plays the melody to Mick Jagger and suggests a line from a Chuck Berry song as the title: "I can't get no satisfaction." In a matter of minutes, Jagger writes a text without thinking — and the song is finished, becoming the first worldwide number-one hit for the Rolling Stones and promoting their stellar rise.

Expressing Jagger's personal dissatisfaction with his life, the song becomes a symbol of the general dissatisfaction of a whole generation. Furthermore, the song explicitly talks about sex, which the older generation in particular regards as an indecent breach of taboos. The Stones are not regarded

as the bad boys of the music world just because of their wild mix of rock 'n' roll and rhythm and blues. In particular, the drug-related excesses of Brian Jones, who drowns in 1969, and riots during their concerts add to their reputation. On September 15, 1965, turmoil breaks out during and after a Stones concert in Berlin. The result: 100 injured people and a destroyed open-air stage, which cannot be used for years.

"Who do you like, the Beatles or the Stones?" becomes a crucial question for millions of young people in the Western world. Both bands are a thorn in the sides of the establishment, but deliberately positioned as opposites by calculating managers, they stand for two different worldviews in the eyes of the public. Good or bad? Just a little bit or truly rebellious? You either favor the suit-wearing, rather intellectual mushroom heads or the scandalous, eccentric group around Mick Jagger, which is considered a true "live band."

In reality, the two bands maintain a good relationship with each other, occasionally even giving performances together, but in the billion-dollar music business, even giants like the Stones and the Beatles need clear-cut profiles in the 1960s. Therefore, the Rolling Stones remain the tougher band, with a sound that is still "rocking" today, in the truest sense of the word.

The Rolling Stones appear on the British TV show "Thank Your Lucky Stars," which is popular among pop music fans from 1961 to 1966.

anarchy and revolt

The Provos stir up the Netherlands

Free cycling for free Dutchmen! Whoever believes that anarchist jokers cannot develop practical, forward-looking concepts is mistaken. In 1965, the artist and political activist Robert Jasper Grootveld introduces the so-called "white bicycle plan" in Amsterdam: All Amsterdammers in the inner city are to be provided with free white bicycles. This is intended to combat the population's new "capitalist" idol — the automobile. The police, however, regard everything the Provos do as aggression and immediately interfere when the first bicycle is painted white. In 1967, a corresponding petition is rejected in the Amsterdam City Council.

Between 1965 and 1967, the barely organized Provos provoke the Amsterdam police with their effective public stunts. Students, artists, and non-conformists, who define themselves as a revolutionary "provotariat," are united less by a common social ideology and more by their discomfort at seeing a prosperous society seemingly freezing in a servile spirit. Their imaginative and humorous provocations are always centered around serious political issues, such as disarmament, the Vietnam War, or women's rights, but to outsiders they often look like theatrical performances or costume festivals. The self-liberation of the individual and of society through art is the utopia of the Provos.

Their goal is to constantly attract state power to the scene by provoking and thus exposing the authoritarian character of society. In fact, the police and the judiciary often react overly harshly. The Provos receive widespread, even international attention on March 16, 1966, when they throw smoke bombs while shouting their battle cry: "Long live the republic!" during the wedding celebrations of Queen Beatrix. The police react extremely harshly, increasing the tension on all sides enormously. A construction workers' riot, also supported by the Provos on June, 13–14, 1966, degenerates into violent street battles with numerous injuries. A year later, the Provo movement breaks up.

But the movement's fight for the bicycle, at least, has had a long-term effect. Today, Amsterdam is considered the bicycle capital of Europe and has an extensive bicycle rental system in the city — although not free of charge.

The wedding of Provo activist Rob Stolk and his 17-year-old girlfriend on October 1, 1965.

the model country of africa

Algeria prospers and acts as a spokescountry for the Third World

After the government's reform measures fail to take effect in the first years of Algeria's independence (see page 38), a power struggle erupts within the governing FLN party. In the end, President Ben Bella is overthrown by his deputy, defense minister Houari Boumedienne, in June 1965.

Boumedienne pursues his vision of an individual path to socialism. Following in the wake of the Soviet Union, but independently and with good economic contacts with the West and with non-aligned states, he increases oil production, nationalizes the oil companies, and uses the revenues to support rapid industrialization by ordering and setting up turnkey factories. He puts his main focus on iron and steel, large companies and conglomerates.

His plan to make Algeria economically independent, however, leads to new dependencies, because food and commodities are imported rather than produced. The cities in the north are growing rapidly as a result of the immigration of industrial workers; the government can barely set up prefabricated buildings and workers' settlements as quickly as they are needed.

Boumedienne's Algerian socialism promotes vocational training for women and their placement in technical professions as well as in traditionally "male domains," such as the military, the police, or as pilots. In the cities, many women are dressed in Western-style clothing.

Boumedienne continues Ben Bella's line of foreign policy and appears as a spokesman for the Third World: Algiers becomes a refuge for guerrilleros fighting against the military dictatorship in Brazil as well as for freedom fighters of Angola and Mozambique, and the headquarters of the U.S. Black Panther movement, which celebrates a colorful Pan-African festival in the streets. At the end of the 1960s, Algeria is on its way to becoming a serious player on the world political stage; this goal will be achieved by the mid-1970s. Leading a legendary fight against personal enrichment, corruption, and waste, the ascetic Boumedienne stands at the height of his reputation, and Algeria becomes a model for the Third World states.

When Boumedienne dies of lymphoma at the early age of 51 in December 1978, he is mourned worldwide. His successor, Chadli Bendjedid, has to reverse some of his measures and is confronted with demonstrations against unemployment as well as housing and consumer goods shortages in the 1980s.

Young women in uniform stand in front of a portrait of Algerian President Houari Boumedienne following a military parade.

a boomtown out of nowhere

Singapore becomes independent

When Singapore declares its independence on August 9, 1965, there is no indication that 50 years later, this island nation will be one of the most important business locations in the Asian region, with more than five and a half million inhabitants. On the contrary: The former British colony, which forms a federation with neighboring Malaysia in 1962, from which it must extricate itself three years later after violent racial riots, lacks everything in the beginning — jobs, raw materials, and housing. Even the fresh water has to be imported from Malaysia (as is still the case today). The island is little more than a big harbor with many warehouses and primitive factories.

Singapore's extreme growth over the following years is basically due to the initiative of one man: The founder of the state, Lee Kuan Yew, puts the country through a rigorous process of development in all areas starting in 1965. The political developments in China and Taiwan play into

his hands, because after Mao's takeover, Western corporations are desperately looking for alternative production locations. So the hard-working, well-managed, cheap labor in Singapore comes just in the nick of time. The city-state starts to specialize in electrical appliances and electronics and establishes a hub in Asian air traffic, eventually becoming a leading commercial center of the financial economy.

But success has its price: Lee, the long-term premier, issues countless restrictive rules about public life, and labor law lags far behind Western standards. Nevertheless, the people stand behind their democratically elected leadership. It takes 20 years for the first opposition party to enter parliament.

View of Singapore in November 1965.

guerrilla war for the poor of south america

Camilo Torres and liberation theology

"Camilo Torres is dead!" — this news shocks Colombia on February 16, 1966, and is heard around the world. One of the most charismatic resistance fighters in South America has perished in an ambush on a military patrol — and his devastated followers wonder how this could actually happen. For Camilo Torres was a priest.

At the time, Colombia has been engaged in a veritable civil war for almost 20 years: Armed guerrilla groups, especially the FARC, are fighting against the brutal suppression of the rural population by the few land barons and the corrupt government, with its death squads. Torres, however, chooses a different path.

After being ordained a priest in 1954, he studies sociology in Europe, where he becomes familiar with the doctrines of Marxism as a student pastor in West Berlin. Returning to Bogotá in 1959, he becomes the co-founder of the sociology faculty at the university and teaches his theories on the compatibility of Christianity and Marxism and their shared struggle against poverty and oppression. "Why should we argue whether the soul is mortal or immortal when we both know that hunger is fatal?"

He becomes increasingly radical, establishes "Christian-Marxist" groups, organizes strike movements, becomes the standard-bearer of the poor and the left-wing students in Colombia, and is soon famous beyond the borders of his country. The living conditions of the rural population and blue-collar workers are similarly catastrophic throughout South America. Courageous priests like Camilo Torres become the voice of the poor and, combining pastoral and practical political work, models for "liberation theologians" operating throughout Latin America from the late 1960s onward, and later even in Africa, Asia, and the U.S.

However, Torres's political agitation angers the church authorities, and he is defrocked in 1965. Threatened and persecuted as the mastermind of Colombia's leftist movements, he joins the armed Marxist National Liberation Army (ELN) and goes underground: "If Jesus were alive today, he would be a guerrillero." Camilo Torres is arrested in February 1966.

Liberation theology remains an important force in the struggle against the oppression of poor populations until the 1990s.

Camilo Torres is enthusiastically greeted by his followers in Bogotá.

the rastafari in jamaica

Reggae rebel Bob Marley and the Rastafarian movement

A head full of tremendous dreadlocks, a joint in his hand, and a faraway look in his eyes. That is the way the whole world knows the Jamaican reggae musician and poet Bob Marley, who thrilled fans from all continents with hits like "I Shot the Sheriff" and "No Woman No Cry."

From the mid-1960s onward, the charismatic singer also becomes the voice of a unique Jamaican anti-authoritarian resistance movement: His songs are closely linked to the messianic religion of the Rastafari, which is common among the socially disadvantaged people of Jamaica, and has many followers especially among the descendants of African slaves. The Rastafari, or Rastas for short, oppose the discrimination and materialism of the white upper class with their own societal model: living together in a faith community in harmony with nature and God.

The name of the religion derives from the birth name of the Ethiopian Emperor Haile Selassie I, whom the Rastafari worship as a messiah. When Haile Selassie visits Jamaica in April 1966, over 100,000 Rastas come to the airport, storming the runway after the plan lands and celebrating their religious leader enthusiastically. Although the emperor does not support the personality cult of the Rastas and advises those who want to immigrate to Ethiopia to be socially and politically active in their own country instead, his official visit to Jamaica puts the Rastafarian movement in the international limelight for a brief moment. Even today, April 21 is celebrated as a Rastafarian holiday.

In 1967, Bob Marley openly commits himself to the religious-political cause of the Rastafari. His songs tell of pain, but also of piety and liberation, of hope and victory. He creates a completely new style of music: Reggae music becomes slower in the late 1960s, not least because of the ritual consumption of marijuana. Mixed with African drums, the fast ska beat develops into the characteristically slow dance rhythm of reggae. Over the following years, the music of Bob Marley, Peter Tosh, Inner Circle, and others goes around the world, expressing the concerns and beliefs of the Rastafari.

Bob Marley during a concert in the late 1960s, with a portrait of Haile Selassie I in the background.

twiggy

A fashion model becomes a style icon

No bust, no butt, skinny arms and legs, and a strict bob haircut instead of long, curly hair: Lesley Hornby differs in every aspect from the curvy beauty queens of the 1950s, à la Marilyn Monroe. It is precisely this difference that turns the barely 16-year-old girl into a shooting star of the British fashion scene overnight, after her photos are published in the *Daily Express* in 1966. Just a few months later, "Twiggy" is on the covers of all of the leading fashion magazines throughout the entire Western world. In the same year, she is nominated for British Woman of the Year.

She is the first supermodel of the world and the perfect icon of the new fashion scene in "Swinging London," which has expanded particularly around Carnaby Street and fashion designer Mary Quant, in competition with the world's fashion capital, Paris (see page 34). Twiggy's androgynous, child-woman look in a daring miniskirt stands for fashion that breaks with old conventions and expresses a new, free approach to life. Away with the strict requirements of traditional gender roles! The young generation experiments with colors, fabrics, and shapes in all directions — anything is allowed.

One of the most eccentric trends of the time is the futuristic fashion emerging in the mid-1960s: Space fashion reflects the space craze, triggered among other things by the first manned space flight of Yuri Gagarin (see page 24). Plastic coats in cream-colored astronaut white and helmet-like hats with vision slits are the latest fad. Designers such as the Spaniard Paco Rabanne or the Frenchman Pierre Cardin are constantly developing new futuristic variants. Knee-high or even waist-high patent leather boots ("space boots") are especially popular among fashion-conscious women. Transparent PVC dresses, on the other hand, seem too daring even for the more adventurous fashionistas and are rarely sighted.

Twiggy's career does not stop at fashion: she performs in theater plays, appears on TV shows and in feature films, sings, records, and poses with pop stars like David Bowie — everything keeps on *swinging* in London, even way after the 1960s.

Twiggy gives the camera one of her typical, long-lashed looks while posing in a mini dress, 1966.

1966

women's liberation

Women fight for a new society

After the Second World War, a period of restoration begins in almost all Western countries: Reconstruction, concentration on economic growth, and concern with political stability are the top priorities. Socially, this goes hand in hand with the ideal of the nuclear family and the barefoot-and-pregnant image of women. Women's emancipation consequently takes a step backward from the understanding of roles developed during the libertine 1920s.

It is not until the 1960s that changes begin to emerge. In 1966, Betty Friedan founds the National Organization for Women (NOW) in the U.S., which is committed to the successive integration of women into the working world as well as to increased political participation. Soon, younger campaigners break away from NOW to take direct actions against concrete grievances. In 1968, feminists disrupt the Miss America pageant, which they decry as a "sexist meat market." Others burn cosmetics and bras, which they see as symbols of male oppression of women.

In the form of many individual associations and movements, the women's liberation movement fights against male dominance in all social areas in the late 1960s. This so-called "second wave of feminism" now also reaches Europe. In England, France, West Germany, the Netherlands, and Scandinavia, women join together and protest for gender equality in the family, in the workplace, in education and training, in all economic matters, and in politics. However, it is a long and difficult road: the political establishment, the conservative press, and civil society largely dismiss and ridicule feminist issues. Even legislative changes that are considered self-evident today take ages. For example, the status of the man as the head of the household who makes all the decisions about family planning, residence, private investments, etc., is abolished in France in 1970, in

Germany in 1977, and in the Netherlands only in 1984. It is particularly scandalous that women in Switzerland do not gain the right to vote until 1971.

From the 1960s onward, the women's movement achieves fundamental progress on the road to equality. It also addresses some issues for the first time that are still being discussed around the world 50 years later: lesbian love, the right to abortion, sexism in advertising and popular culture, sexual harassment in society, and violence in partnerships.

A young woman throws her bra into a trash can during a demonstration for women's liberation.

1966

1966 USA

black panthers

The struggle against racial oppression

The nonviolent civil rights movement of Martin Luther King Jr. (see page 62) fails to live up to socio-political expectations, which further increases the frustration and disappointment in many black communities in the mid-1960s. Starting in 1966, diverse cultural-political currents gather under the slogan Black Power — some with a nationalist, others with a more socialist orientation — all with one goal in common: Segregation from white society and the shaping of a unique African-American self-consciousness ("black is beautiful").

In reaction to severe police violence toward black people, two college students, Huey P. Newton and Bobby Seale, found the "Black Panther Party" in California in 1966, initially as an armed militia. The organization soon founds local chapters in many large U.S. cities. Dressed in black leather jackets and militant berets and usually armed, they patrol black neighborhoods and monitor the

police, which frequently leads to shootings. Following the socialist-revolutionary ideas of Malcolm X (see page 74), the Panthers see themselves as fighters in the global struggle for increased social justice. Their educational and social programs in particular strongly increase their popularity in black ghettoes. The Black Power activist Angela Davis is a prominent advocate of the Black Panthers and briefly even becomes a member in 1969.

However, the Black Panthers' uprising against the system also includes violence, which makes the movement "the greatest threat to the country's internal security" according to FBI chief J. Edgar Hoover. The government infiltrates the organization with agents and does not shy away from targeted killings. The intensified conflicts with the state after the assassination of Martin Luther King Jr. in 1968 wear the organization down. Internal disruptions finally lead to the demise of the Black

Panthers in 1971.

Were they consistent freedom fighters for minorities or mostly violent criminals? Up to the present day, the Black Panthers are judged in very different ways in the U.S. However, at least one nonviolent protest salute gains worldwide attention: the African-American U.S. athletes Tommie Smith and John Carlos raise their clenched fists in black gloves during their awards ceremony at the 1968 Olympic Games in Mexico to signal their solidarity with the Black Power movement, thereby causing an international scandal.

A chapter of the Black Panthers stands outside the New York City courthouse during a hearing.

1966 SPAIN

freedom under franco

The spark of international protest jumps to dictatorial Spain

After the Spanish Civil War, from 1939 onward, General Francisco Franco established a dictatorial regime, based on his personality cult and supported by the police, the military, and the Catholic Church. He stifled regional efforts at independence and immediately disrupted occasional labor unrest, strikes, and the activities of illegal unions that followed the great socialist and anarchist tradition of Spain prior to 1939. In this way, he created total domestic stagnation.

When the censorship of the press is eased in 1966, largely apolitical Spaniards first learn about student protests and civil rights activists in other countries. In the same year, 500 student representatives meet in Barcelona and found an illegal student council. The police break up the meeting and arrest the leading activists. Then something completely unexpected happens: 60,000 industrial workers and 2,300 railroad workers join the students in a solidarity strike. Simple

parish priests join in solidarity with the workers, and finally, in 1968, even the Spanish episcopal conference demands the free election of workers' representatives and the right to strike. Over the following years, parts of the student body become radicalized, storming university institutes and directorates and attacking representatives of the regime. Several universities are threatening to slip out of the government's control. The spark of the student revolution has seemingly jumped from the U.S. and other parts of Europe to Spain, and liberalization is within reach.

However, Franco is still sitting firmly in the saddle. On January 24, 1969, he declares a state of emergency throughout Spain and speaks of actions targeted against public order: "This cold strategy shamelessly exploits the naivety and generosity of the youth to throw them into an orgy of anarchy, nihilism and disobedience."

In Madrid alone, 400 students as well as several professors,

lawyers, and trade unionists are arrested, with up to 3,000 more people apprehended nationwide. Books by leftist authors, from Marx to Marcuse, disappear from the libraries, and critical plays are banned. Lecturers are encouraged to spy on their students, prevent student meetings, and denounce "suspicious" students to the police. The press is forcibly coordinated; there is strict censorship. Until Franco's death in November 1975, there are no further significant protests by students or democrats in Spain.

Hundreds of citizens take part in a spontaneous demonstration on November 30, 1968, on the Ramblas in Barcelona after a service in the Belén Church. Shortly after the protesters reach Gracia Avenue, the rally dissolves on its own.

the "great chairman" explains the world

The Little Red Book becomes a cult object

Just like the Christian Bible in the past, a small booklet bound with a red cover spreads around the world in the 1960s, becoming commonly known in the West as the "Little Red Book."

After overcoming harsh criticism within the party, Mao Tse-tung, Chairman of the Communist Party of China, begins to establish a personality cult around himself in 1964. The *Quotations from Chairman Mao Tse-tung* compile 427 quotes from his writings, essays, and speeches, divided into 33 chapters. Among other things, they deal with the Party, class struggle, and the "People's War"; the army, education, and the development of the country; cadres, youth, and women; research, culture, and art; criticism and self-criticism. Originally issued for the education of the "People's Liberation Army," the book becomes the Bible of the revolutionary Red Guards, who carry it along on their missions and quote from it during the Mao-initiated Cultural

Revolution starting in 1966. The very first page reads: "Study Chairman Mao's writings, follow his teachings, and act according to his instructions." This turns Mao into a "classic" of Marxism-Leninism.

The planned export of the Little Red Book begins in 1967: The work is translated into numerous languages and delivered to publishers in 117 countries, allegedly adding up to several billion copies. Harboring romantic notions about Mao's isolated empire, student movements of the Western world avidly absorb the book and use quotes and slogans for their own struggle. In this way, Mao's description of imperialism as a "paper tiger" becomes popular in the West and is applied to dominant institutions, which seem terrifying but are "nothing" in reality.

Apart from isolated Maoists, however, the majority must recognize that many passages are specifically tailored to China and serve to justify the

millions of victims that the "Great Leap Forward" has left behind. Initially, Western revolutionaries also welcome the Cultural Revolution, which rages between 1966 and 1969, as Mao propagates it: as a revolt and as the youth's self-liberation from bureaucracy and corrupt cadres. The destruction of centuries-old cultural artifacts and the brutal humiliation of teachers and intellectuals is not mentioned.

Even activists who promote armed struggle in the early 1970s do not refer to the Little Red Book. Readers are able to discern a "flaw" in 1971. The preface is written by Mao's chosen successor, Lin Biao, who dares to revolt in 1971, dies under mysterious circumstances, and whose story has been hushed up ever since. In China, everyone who owns the Little Red Book is instructed to tear out his preface.

Teenagers recite excerpts from Mao's Little Red Book at a rally in Beijing.

the detroit race riot

Discrimination and segregation threaten the future of every American

Although the media focus of the Civil Rights movement of the 1960s was centered in the South where segregation and bigotry were openly a part of the society, African Americans in the major cities in the North were often distinctly second-class citizens. The Detroit riot on July 23, 1967 followed a similar deadly riot in Newark, New Jersey only a few weeks earlier.

The cause of both riots, and of the despair and alienation that lay behind them, was deeply rooted in the institution of slavery that had only been abolished barely 100 years ago. In addition to this legacy, African Americans in the industrial cities of the North found themselves trapped in inner cities that were fast becoming economic wastelands as downtown industry moved to the suburbs. As the jobs disappeared, so did the white population and the unemployment rate among those left behind soared.

Detroit's police department, then overwhelmingly white, like those in Chicago and many other major cities, had a culture of discrimination against African Americans who viewed them as an occupying army rather than a police force.

The Detroit riot started when police raided an after-hours club at 3:30 AM on 12th Street, an overwhelmingly African American neighborhood. Hundreds of people were still awake and on the streets at this late hour, seeking relief from the heat wave that gripped the city. As the police arrested the patrons of the club a few onlookers threw bottles and bricks at the police cars. The situation quickly escalated in violence and the police lost control of larger and larger areas of the city as they erupted in looting and arson.

In the week between July 23 and 28 the State Police, then the Michigan National Guard and finally US Army paratroopers were called out to help the police keep order and stop the rioting. More than 7000 people were arrested, more than 43 killed and more than 300 injured. By the time it was over, tanks patrolled the streets and over 1400 buildings had been burned, many of which would never be rebuilt.

After the riot, President Johnson established the Kerner Commission. The months of study revealed what the riots had made overwhelmingly obvious: "Our nation is moving toward two societies, one black, one white – separate and unequal. Reaction to last summer's disorders has quickened the movement and deepened the division. Discrimination and segregation have long permeated much of American life; they now threaten the future of every American."

Piles of rubble left after stores and houses were damaged after the riot.

1967 WEST GERMANY

a gunshot radicalizes the student movement

The murder of Benno Ohnesorg in Berlin

When the Shah of Persia arrives at the Deutsche Oper in Berlin-Charlottenburg on the evening of June 2, the confrontation between protesters and the police escalates once again. The authorities are ruthlessly taking action against the leftist opponents of the Shah with billy clubs and water canons, when suddenly a gunshot goes off around 8:20 p.m. in the backyard of a side street. The student Benno Ohnesorg collapses, fatally wounded. The gunman, the police officer Karl-Heinz Kurras, later claims to have acted in self-defense. He is acquitted at the court trial. Today's evidence, however, reveals that there were false witness statements and attempts by the police to cover up the truth.

Ohnesorg's death and, above all, the authorities' dubious handling of the incident shock critical minds nationwide and strengthen the radical student faction around the Berlin leader of the Socialist German Student Union (SDS), Rudi Dutschke.

Is the state now really on the way to a new fascism, if it will even tolerate the deaths of demonstrators?

On the evening of Ohnesorg's funeral, a ferocious debate takes place in Hanover between Rudi Dutschke and the philosopher Jürgen Habermas about the legitimacy of violence in the struggle against the system. Like Dutschke, more and more people advocate acts of violence against objects as self-defense. Both sides strongly step up their rhetoric, fueling further polarization.

The uncomprehending German tabloids, overtly hostile and indiscriminating, agitate against the "red gangs" and their ringleaders. At congresses and demonstrations, on the other hand, participants aggressively preach the "breach of capitalist rules" in order to expose the system as a "dictatorship of violence."

When Dutschke is seriously injured in an assassination attempt on April 11, 1968, days of violent clashes between the police and the left follow, particularly directed against Springer press. Throughout Europe, student leaders declare their solidarity with Dutschke. As a further consequence, militant left-wing extremists go underground in Germany. They found the terrorist group 2 June Movement and finally the Red Army Faction (RAF), which commits terror attacks and murders in the 1970s and, in some cases, even into the 1990s (see page 197).

Twenty minutes after he is shot in the head by a police officer, the student Benno Ohnesorg is lifted into an ambulance. He dies during the ride to the hospital.

what do I want today?

Anti-authoritarian children's shops and Summerhill revolutionize education

Tricycles, chairs, and other furniture are piled up in a heap, and the walls are painted with bright colors: In many kindergartens in West Germany, and especially in West Berlin, things look pretty wild and creative by the end of the 1960s. Where discipline and subordination once ruled, everything has suddenly become freer and more easygoing. Particularly in West Germany, newly founded "children's shops" (Kinderläden) experiment with modern models of education that are supposed to encourage the development of critical faculties, self-determination, and self-awareness in children. Not simply doing what one is told to do, but learning to know what one wants to do is the new emancipatory principle of education, which understands itself as a consequence of the dark German past. In this way, educators want to prevent the further development of the so-called "authoritarian character" which, according to the German philosopher Theodor Adorno, made National Socialism possible in the first place.

In 1967, Monika Seifert founds the alternative Children's School in Frankfurt, which will become the model for many other children's shops over the next few years. Helke Sander, chairwoman of the Action Council for the Liberation of Women, initiates the first children's shop in West Berlin in 1968. There are soon two different approaches: For some, anti-authoritarian education is part of a socio-revolutionary struggle, in which children are to be trained to resist oppressive systems. The Central Council for Socialist Children's Shops in West Berlin, for example, discusses this type of indoctrination. For others, the "anti" of education is not primarily resistance to external authorities, but rather liberation from internalized obedience to authorities. In this sense, this attitude is less "anti" than "pro" — namely, in favor of children's free development.

The transition is fluid, but above all, liberal educational principles are encouraged after the stories and theories of the educator A.S. Neill are published in Germany: At his private school Summerhill on the English east coast, he practices education without forced learning and punishment. His system and has been recognized in England, the U.S., and even in traditionally authoritarian Japan.

In Germany, the anti-authoritarian spirit prevails as a younger generation of educators grows up in the 1970s. Today, central educational goals such as a child's autonomy and an orientation toward the well-being of the child have long been generally recognized.

Creative chaos at the Frankfurt "children's shop" in the late 1960s.

1967 USA

free life under open skies

Countryside communes as a trend and ecstatic adventure

Finding inner peace and drawing strength from nature and community with others is the philosophy of the musician Lou Gottlieb, who founds the Morningstar Commune in California in 1967. Models of this lifestyle can be found in the history of early American settlers and among 18th- and 19th-century pietists, but Indian ashrams are extremely "in" at this time. Getting out of the city, away from consumerism — many young people who have experimented with new forms of living in San Francisco's Haight-Ashbury district embark on the so-called Hippie Trail to India from the mid-1960s onward (see page 140) or found communes based on free love, small farming, and drug use in the countryside. Everyone is welcome to join, since after all, this is "God's own country." This can cause trouble with the authorities. The Morningstar Commune is bulldozed and rebuilt three times before finally failing in 1973.

As early as 1965, art students found the first rural hippie commune — Drop City in Colorado — which presents itself as a movement of ongoing art production. Influenced by the geodesic domes of the architect Buckminster Fuller, the residents build tent-like, futuristic dwellings from the sheet metal of old cars and challenge American teenagers to "tear the top off your daddy's car, and send it, together with 10 cents in cash or coin, to Drop City, Colorado." Regular spectacles attract hundreds of visitors. New communities and artist initiatives break away from the commune. In 1977, the authorities close down the experiment, and the last sheet metal dome goes to a scrap dealer.

As the "ultimate hippie fantasy," Taylor Camp is set up in 1969 by 13 hippies sentenced to community service against the breathtaking backdrop of the Hawaiian island of Kauai. Around 300 seekers and draft dodgers come here to walk around naked, grow marijuana, and practice free sex. Since they are not allowed to build ground dwellings, they live in homemade treehouses. In 1974, the state puts an end to their peaceful activities, the last remaining residents are evicted in 1977, and their tree houses are burned down.

Although rural communes are still rare in the 1960s, they already anticipate a trend: After a decade of protests and counterculture, many people — not just in the U.S. — withdraw from the cities in the 1970s to seek a self-determined life in the countryside. In some cases, this leads to new communes, such as the famous settlement Christiania, a district of Copenhagen, which still survives today.

Communards construct a geodesic dome out of auto sheet metal at the Drop City commune.

1967 USA

the summer of love

The utopia of love and social integration

In the beginning, only a few hippies form the counterculture around the Bay Area of San Francisco. They wear colorful tie-dye clothing, smoke joints or take LSD trips, and hang flowers around their necks. "Flower Power" is born. Especially in the area around Haight and Ashbury streets in San Francisco an alternative, more peaceful way of life is tested, directed against the killing in Vietnam and particularly against consumer-oriented prosperity and meritocracy — the American way of life.

In the summer of 1967, 100,000 hippies from all over the world, but predominantly from the U.S., flock to parks in the neighboring villages and spend weeks celebrating the birth of a "new world (of love)." There are readings, street theater, and music performances everywhere. No form of art is too crazy to go public. People sleep in parks for weeks, open living communities emerge, and food and clothing are exchanged at so-called swap shops. Materialism and violence are to be replaced by love, music, and peace, creating a new, harmonious togetherness. The highlight of the summer is a big music festival in Monterey from June 16–18, where up to 90,000 people cheer rock stars like Jimi Hendrix and The Who and get high. Everything is free and seemingly boundless. The "Summer of Love" is also a big media event, either glorified or, usually, vilified. Through media reports, hippie culture gradually penetrates mass culture.

Overwhelmed by all the events, the San Francisco police declare the end of the "Freak Summer" in September 1967. On October 6, 1967, followers in Haight-Ashbury symbolically carry a hippie coffin to its grave. The "Summer of Love" is over, although its epilogue, the legendary Woodstock Festival, is yet to come.

Dancing hippies at an open-air event during the summer of 1967.

new hollywood

Popular cinema discovers social criticism

A young man standing at the threshold casts a timid glance at a woman's long leg stretched out in an erotic pose. This is probably the most famous scene from Mike Nichols's movie *The Graduate*, which marks not only the start of Dustin Hoffman's international career, but is also one of the first films of "New Hollywood."

The story of a clumsy college graduate who maintains a forbidden relationship with a mature, married woman and transforms from a good, bourgeois boy into a rebel has little to do with the classic, escapist Hollywood plots, but everything to do with the new spirit of change. The movie satirizes not only the moral standards of the establishment, but also the inhibitions of the younger generation — all of this accompanied by the songs of Simon and Garfunkel, which in turn become international hits thanks to this movie.

With its outmoded historical epics and established star structure, classic Hollywood cinema is incapable of reaching a young audience. Instead, the second half of the 1960s sees the emergence of a new generation of filmmakers telling unconventional, outsider stories and practicing social criticism. Following the example of French Nouvelle Vague auteurs (see page 16), they rely on unconventional camera shots, realistic plots and settings, and are often involved in the filmmaking process from scripting to editing.

Released at the same time as *The Graduate*, the gangster drama *Bonnie and Clyde* attracts considerable attention. The controversial movie aestheticizes the historical criminal couple's self-destructive struggle against social conventions with unusual screen violence.

In the late 1960s, the mockumentary *Take the Money and Run* marks the beginning of Woody Allen's career. The intellectual U.S. comedian creates a completely new comic genre with bizarre wordplay and imagery and neurotic anti-heroes.

Released in 1969, *Easy Rider* is the most successful and probably the most characteristic film of the New Hollywood era. This road movie about two outlaws on motorcycles tells the classic hippie story of freedom and adventure beyond bourgeois lifestyles, without — and this is new — romanticizing their dark side of violence and drug excesses.

In The Graduate, *Benjamin Braddock (Dustin Hoffman) is seduced by a friend of his parents.*

1967 USA

march on the pentagon

The anti-Vietnam protest reaches its first climax

Late on October 21, 1967, a brutal showdown takes place in front of the Ministry of Defense in Washington, D.C. On the one hand, the radical opponents of the U.S. intervention in Vietnam; on the other, heavily armed Marines. The government has requested military troops to protect the ministry for the first time in decades. As protesters try to enter the Pentagon, federal authorities use tear gas and batons. Approximately 600 demonstrators are arrested.

This is the sad end of an impressive demonstration with an absolutely peaceful beginning. At the height of the nationwide week of protest against President Johnson's Vietnam policy, more than 100,000 people gather (on the initiative of more than 150 peace groups) in front of the Lincoln Memorial in the morning to hold the largest anti-war demonstration to date. A colorful coalition of leftist liberals, left-wing radicals, hippies, pastors, professors, and students demands an immediate end to the bombing and the withdrawal of all troops from South Vietnam. For three years, the U.S. has been sending more and more soldiers (and war material) to the Southeast Asian jungle state without any substantial success. Leftist demonstrators chant in choruses: "Hell no, we won't go!" Banners read: "Johnson is a war criminal." Hippies sing protest songs and give flowers to the troops.

This hardly changes the strict pro-government attitude of many media outlets toward the Vietnam War. Many conservative commentators believe that they are facing a hateful, pro-communist mob riot. Large sections of the population still consider it their patriotic duty to unconditionally support their own soldiers on the "home front." American society is deeply divided, and the gaps have been widening for months.

The North Vietnamese Tet Offensive in 1968 becomes a turning point in the public perception of the war (see page 146), as the prospect of a U.S. victory recedes into the distance. After this event, the majority of the U.S. population advocates an end to the war.

Confrontation between demonstrators and the military police in front of the Pentagon on October 21, 1967.

the myth of che guevara

An Argentine revolutionary becomes an international icon

Vallegrande, October 10, 1967. Ernesto Che Guevara, the chief ideologist of the Cuban Revolution of 1959, a guerrilla fighter plotting revolutions in other Latin American countries since 1965, is lying in front of the international press in the washroom of the local hospital. He is dead, killed by soldiers in Bolivia, where he and his troops had been fighting their way through the forests for months without success.

The documentation of his final defeat launches a myth: With his eyes open, his seemingly intrepid facial expression, and his long, curly hair and beard, the dead Che eerily resembles the dead body of Jesus Christ taken from the cross.

As it circulates worldwide, this photograph strengthens the image of a superhuman hero that Che already possessed during his lifetime, embodying the leftist spirit of the 1960s like no other. At no other time would the death of an unsuccessful, violent guerrilla fighter have found such resonance.

The idea of "Jesus with gun" as Wolf Biermann called him gains ground throughout Latin America and Europe. His heroic deeds are glorified in songs, texts, and pictures. No leftist demonstration in Western Europe is complete without the image of the fearless Comandante Che. For many, he becomes a projection surface for their own yearnings for change and their struggles for a good and just cause, although this is often a rather self-righteous approach. Che is elevated to the status of an ideal "new man," an image which he himself had propagated as an aspiration: a man acting on a moral incentive in his work for the community and not for material self-interest; a man sacrificing himself to build a better and more just society, unselfish and uncompromising until the end.

As rumor has it, his last words are: "Shoot, coward, you are only going to kill a man!" In the end, it is his "heroic" death rather than the deeds of his life that turns Che Guevara into an immortal legend.

The military chief shows the bullet wound in Che Guevara's dead body to journalists on October 10, 1967.

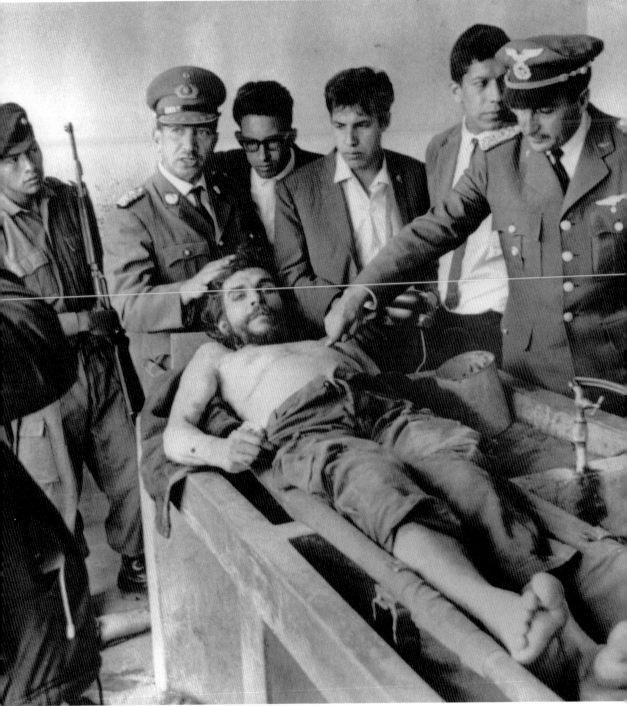

1967 JAPAN

the power of the zengakuren

A Japanese student league enters politics

Unlike the student protests in many other countries, those in Japan do not suddenly break out in the 1960s; they have a longer history. It begins in 1948, with the founding of the Zengakuren, the All-Japan League of Student Self-Government. After the Second World War, this socialist-oriented student league protested against the planned privatization of the universities, the allegiance with the U.S., and the Korean War. It brought university life to a standstill with mass strikes.

The next major action of the Zengakuren begins in 1960. In May, activists storm parliament to prevent the ratification of the U.S.-Japan Security Treaty, which binds Japan firmly to the West. In June, 5.8 million students and workers take to the streets again for the same cause. Zengakuren activists storm Haneda Airport, causing the cancellation of U.S. President Eisenhower's visit, as well as the University of Tokyo campus. One student dies, and over 500 are injured. In July, the Kishi government resigns.

Over the following years, the Zengakuren splits into various Marxist groups and organizes protest campaigns against the superpowers' nuclear weapon tests. During the mid-1960s, the Zengakuren try to form a joint party with young workers' organizations, and both take the lead in the protests against the Vietnam War. Protest marches, rallies, and strikes are the order of the day.

In October 1967, about a thousand militant Zengakuren activists, experienced in street fighting and armed with helmets and bamboo poles, storm Haneda Airport again to prevent Prime Minister Sato's trip to South Vietnam. In a ruthless battle with the police forces, one student dies and 600 are injured. The Zengakuren celebrate the airport occupation as "the birth of a new left in Japan" because more and more groups join the protests against the Vietnam War.

However, the protest also revolves around national problems: through rapid industrialization, Japan

advances to become the third-strongest industrial nation in 1968. The Zengakuren support small farmers' protests against their expropriation for the construction of industrial plants and major airports and also stage protests against massive environmental pollution.

To this day, Zengakuren groups still organize protest movements on all relevant social issues, both at home and abroad.

Radical left-wing Zengakuren students demonstrate against the construction of the airport in Tokyo.

1967

a sensation on the operating table

The first heart transplant opens up new dimensions for humanity

On December 3, 1967, the history of medicine is being rewritten at the Groote Schuur Hospital in Cape Town. With his 30-person team, the South African surgeon Christiaan Barnard conducts the first heart transplant. The patient, 53-year-old Louis Washkansky, introduced to the international press for the first time with his full name and photo, is doing well after the operation but succumbs to pneumonia 18 days later, because his immune system was deliberately weakened to avoid organ rejection. But for the international press it is clear that Barnard has "opened the door to new dimensions in medicine."

Of course, this milestone is not reached overnight. Since the beginning of the 20th century, medical pioneers have worked in the field of organ transplantation. The first heart transplant, performed on a dog in 1905, and the first kidney transplant, performed on a human in 1933, both failed because of organ rejection.

After the discovery of tissue compatibility and immune response in 1944, as well as the development of drugs to suppress rejection by the early 1960s, organ transplants were performed with increasing success. Yet, prior to Washkansky, nobody had ever survived a heart transplant.

Barnard's second patient, 58-year-old Philip Blaiberg, undergoes a heart transplant on January 2, 1968, survives for 18 months — until August 1969 — and writes an autobiography. His fate is considered a once-in-a-century success.

In 1974, Barnard is also the first to implant a healthy donor heart to support the patient's diseased heart (a so-called "piggyback transplant"). He becomes a favorite member of the jet set, lectures worldwide, and meets the greats in politics, science, and show business. The South African apartheid regime consciously ignores the significant contribution his black lab assistant, Hamilton Naki, makes to his work.

The hype leads to 100 heart transplants worldwide in 1968, but it soon becomes apparent that the long-term survival rate of heart transplant patients is not very good. As early as 1969, worldwide transplants are cut down to 53, and the number drops to 30 in 1970. Of the 164 transplant patients operated on during this time, only 20 are still alive in September 1970. Long-term transplant successes are not common until the mid-80s. Today, more than 100,000 heart transplants have been performed worldwide.

Dr. Christiaan Barnard is surrounded by reporters in London on May 7, 1968.

science as an anarcho-experiment

The Anti-University of London

To develop truly free-thinking and revolutionary ideas beyond government guidelines and subsidies as an answer to the intellectual bankruptcy and spiritual emptiness of educational institutions in England and the rest of the Western world. This is the goal of the "Anti-University," founded in London in February 1968 by Allen Krebs, David Cooper, and Joseph Berke, thereby unhinging the entire academic world.

These left-wing U.S. academic rebels want to create the theoretical foundations for a society based on the values of humanity and exchange. The ideals of a commune are to be transferred to a new society.

Everything — or almost everything — at the "counter-university" differs from conventional universities: Seminars are not held in historic, elegant buildings but in the rooms of a worn-out warehouse in the dingy London district of Shoreditch. There are no exams and no degrees. The clear line between teachers and students is also eliminated. Anyone can take on the role of discussion leader, and any issue can be addressed — from the benefits and drawbacks of LSD trips, to the meaning of anti-institutions, to the psychological dilemma of self-alienation. Rules are out, methods follow the happy, anarchistic principle of "anything goes," and joints are often passed around among the participants.

In the end, the intellectual experiment fails for a profane reason: the lack of money. This chaotic playground of rule-free discourse is closed at the beginning of 1969.

The London Anti-University is not unique. A year earlier, so-called "critical universities" are founded, or rather proclaimed within existing universities in Germany. Unlike the antiquated university system in which "nerd professors educate nerd students," critical lectures aim to use "critical-theoretical reflection and empirical-analytical methods to contribute to the determination of the goals and actions of the non-parliamentary radical-democratic opposition groups in West Berlin," as the first course catalogue of the Berlin Critical University explains in exaggerated terms typical of the time.

The critical universities also die out quickly in Germany. Not only is there a lack of funds and organizational structures, but also — and most importantly — of interested students.

Poster for the founding semester of the London Anti-University.

1968

ANTIUNIVERSITY OF LONDON

OPENING FEBRUARY 12th, 1968

FACULTY INCLUDES:

STEVE ABRAMS	ALLEN GINSBERG	JULIET MITCHELL
KOSTAS AXELOS	RICHARD HAMILTON	STUART MONTGOMERY
ROY BATTERSBY	JIM HAYNES	ROLAND MULDOON
ASA BENVENISTA	ADRIAN HENRY	AAGE NEILSON
JOSEPH BERKE	CALVIN HERNTON	HAROLD NORSE
ROBIN BLACKBURN	FRANCIS HUXLEY	JEFF NUTTALL
WILLIAM BURROUGHS	C. L. R. JAMES	CEDRIC PRICE
MALCOLM CALDWELL	AXEL JENSEN	AUBREY RAYMOND
CORNELIUS CARDEW	JOHN KEYS	LEON REDLER
STOKELEY CARMICHEL	NICHOLAS KRASSO	JOSEPH ROSENSTEIN
DAVID CAUTE	ALLIN KREBS	THEODORE ROSZAK
KEN COATES	MIKE KUSTOW	MONTY SCHATZMAN
NOEL COBB	BRUCE KUCKLICK	CAROLEE SCHNEEMANN
BOB COBBINCS	R. D. LAING	SUSAN SHERMAN
DAVID COOPER	JOHN LATHAM	TONY SMYTHE
JOHN COWLEY	JIROME LISS	RUSS STETLER
JIME DINE	ANNA LOCKWOOD	PAUL SWEEZY
ED DORN	CHARLES MAROVITZ	IRVING TEITELBAUM
STEVE DWOSKIN	DIONYS MASCOLO	HARRY TREVOR
OBI EGBUNA	HARVEY MATUSOW	ALEXANDER TROCCHI
H. M. EMZEMBERGER	DAVID MERCER	SIMON VINKENOOG
BARRY FLANNAGAN	MILES	JESSE WATKINS

NO FORMAL REQUIREMENTS

139

flower children on a journey to self-discovery

Wild and free on the hippie trail

Beginning in the middle of the 1960s, more and more young people in the USA and Europe, but also in Australia and Japan, want to escape bourgeois constraints and the social pressure to succeed and consume in search of a meaningful way of life. In particular, the Beatles' six-week stay in India to visit Maharishi Mahesh Yogi in February and March of 1968, which receives widespread media attention, makes spiritual teachings from the Far East popular among young people in the West. They too want to seek their paths to inner enlightenment through immersion in Hindu meditation centers.

For this purpose, they embark on the so-called "Hippie Trail" — an overland journey from Europe to Afghanistan or India, which they make by hitchhiking or in the legendary VW bus. Less remote destinations, such as Ibiza and Morocco, are added later.

However, it is perhaps not always spiritual renewal that makes these seekers pack their backpacks. Not even every Beatle manages to endure days of singing Hindu hymns and brooding over Sanskrit words — after a few days, Ringo Starr drops out because of the strict alcohol ban and flies back to London.

Many young people are primarily motivated by a lust for adventure and the search for a simple, original lifestyle. And last but not least, some are just looking forward to the possibility of consuming much cheaper drugs in the "growing areas."

Hippie tourism creates its own infrastructure at the typical way stations — especially in Istanbul, Tehran, Kabul, Bangkok, and Kathmandu. Kabul alone has more than 400 hotels and cheap accommodation for tens of thousands of hippies passing through each year. In Kathmandu, the so-called Freak Street is a popular meeting point, and in Ibiza, everyone goes to the hippie market Las Dalias.

Once in India, often in the state of Goa, many hippies either join one of the Hindu ashram communities for weeks or months or find their own emigrant villages.

Many returnees later open oriental shops in the West or enrich the music, fashion, and art scenes with their own creations, shaped by their travel experiences. As the first big individual travel trend, "hippie tourism" is the forerunner of the "backpacking tourism" of the following decades, which endures even today.

A hippie from Boston on a rowboat on the Ganges River near the city of Benares, India.

1968

sexual revolution

From marital sex to free love — and back

The fact that, prior to the 1960s, men and women wait quite a while before they have sex is not only due to rigid, often religiously based sexual morals. It is also the constant threat of pregnancy that makes pre-marital sex so dangerous.

The development of the birth control pill (see page 14) is therefore regarded as a great liberation in Western countries. It allows the separation of sex and reproduction and thus a fearless sex life. Sex literally becomes a pleasurable diversion, which also results in a rapid revolution in relationship models. Many partnerships are now shorter and less committed, and people change their partners more often and try out new things. "Who-ever sleeps with the same person twice already belongs to the establishment" — this German slogan from the sexual liberation movement is also a challenge to the traditional form of cohabitation — marriage.

After the prudish 1950s, the young generation of the 1960s in the West also develops a freer sexual morality. Nakedness no longer needs to be mythologically "covered," and eroticism is not automatically regarded as obscene. Physical desire is freed from taboos and, at the same time, perceived as an emancipatory political statement against a philistine society. "Free love" is the buzzword of the time, but in nevertheless remains a utopia rather than a lived reality.

Of course, sexual liberation is not left only to the young and progressive. More conventional citizens are also curious and develop a new sexual awareness. In Germany, for example, Oswalt Kolle's sex education films, which are intended to improve marital intimacy with scientific meticulousness, cause quite a stir. As early as 1962, the entrepreneur Beate Uhse opens a "speciality store for marital hygiene," the world's first sex shop, in Flensburg. Despite fierce resistance from the local population, new Beate Uhse stores soon open throughout the country, selling all sorts of stimulating items.

Since the 1950s, the sober, scientific "Kinsey Reports" by the sex researcher Alfred Kinsey have raised public interest in the taboo topic of sex in the USA. They create vigorous controversies — and are eagerly read by millions in the absence of other sex education literature.

Artists, filmmakers, and journalists react quickly and push the boundaries of what may be shown in public. To this day, sexuality (and thus also pornography) remains one of the most sensitive indicators for the liberalization of a society.

The German fashion model and actress Uschi Obermaier also became an iconic sex symbol in the USA through her affairs with Mick Jagger, Keith Richards, and Jimi Hendrix.

1968

1968 USA

2001: A Space Odyssey

The ultimate space experience, courtesy of Stanley Kubrick

Fully dependent on technology, the astronaut Dave Bowman embarks on a journey into the vastness of space, from which he will never return. In the science fiction movie *2001: A Space Odyssey*, the director Stanley Kubrick condenses major socio-cultural themes of the 1960s like rays through a magnifying glass: faith in (not only technical) progress and an almost mythical search for new boundaries and a new consciousness. All of this is wrapped into a rather thin plot that contemplatively tells the story of six astronauts who are sent on a mission to Jupiter in 2001, with the help of an omnipotent computer, to investigate the mysterious signals of an extraterrestrial entity.

This enigmatic space opera is the major cinematic event of the year in 1968, inspiring not only critics, but also viewers. Although the movie's style and content are more like an avant-garde meditation than a popular Hollywood spectacle, it is also commercially successful.

Even today, this philosophical cinematic work is open to multiple interpretations and has lost little of its appeal. The American Film Institute recognized *2001* as the best science fiction film of all time in 2008.

Above all, it is the combination of captivating pictorial compositions and the epic classical music by György Ligeti and Johann and Richard Strauss that creates a visual cinematic experience that is not unintentionally reminiscent of the hallucinatory images evoked by an LSD trip. Linear logic is replaced by feelings and sensations that express dissolution and spirituality.

Various characters and scenes in the movie have become frequently adapted and quoted icons. For instance, the onboard computer, HAL-9000, is the first disembodied villain to enter film history and stands for the new power of technology. Kubrick also introduces pioneering special effects: In one of the most famous match-cuts in filmmaking history, a bone thrown into the air by an ape is transformed into a spaceship — symbolically bridging millions of years of human history, from the dawn of humanity to technological progress.

Man is alone — not only in space, but also in the midst of the technology he has created. A scene from the movie 2001: A Space Odyssey.

1968 VIETNAM

the tet offensive and the my lai massacre

Horror images of the war lead to worldwide mass protests

While the USA is increasing its air strikes in 1967–68, and while the perfidious "body count" (the proof of the number of enemies killed that is required for the promotion of a U.S. soldier) even leads to the killing of civilians, the North Vietnamese People's Army changes its combat strategy. After following Mao's guerrilla tactics in advancing into the rural areas of the south, General Vo Nguyen Giap prepares to conquer the cities with surprise attacks in June 1967. Supported by South Vietnamese underground fighters (Vietcong), he attacks U.S. troops in Khe Sanh in January 1968. U.S. fighter jets retaliate by dropping 100,000 tons of bombs on the surrounding area. But the attack was only a diversionary tactic.

On January 31, 1968, North Vietnam begins the Tet Offensive, a simultaneous attack on several cities in South Vietnam. In Saigon, communist fighters advance on the U.S. embassy. The U.S. Army, which is completely surprised despite having been warned, is involved in endless house-to-house fighting. By March, 14,000 civilians have died, including 6,000 in Saigon alone; 370,000 people are left homeless, and several cities are completely destroyed.

During the battle for Saigon, one of the most famous and disturbing images of the Vietnam War is taken on February 1, 1968: the shooting of a captured Vietcong fighter by the Saigon police chief on the open road, right in front of the camera.

From a position of strength, North Vietnam offers to negotiate with the USA in April, which leads to a gradual withdrawal of the U.S. military from Vietnam. Yet prior to this, U.S. troops, roused by the Tet Offensive, commit a horrific massacre that definitively repudiates this war. On March 16, 1968, soldiers of the 11th Infantry Brigade search the South Vietnamese village of My Lai for hidden Vietcong, but find only women, children, and old men. In a killing frenzy, they rape the women and then kill almost all the villagers — about 500 civilians of all ages. A U.S. helicopter pilot finally puts a stop to their actions by threatening to shoot his "comrades" with his onboard machine gun if they do not stop the slaughter. The army command tries everything to cover up the massacre, referring to a "trip to Pinkville" (the U.S. Army nickname for My Lai). It is only an article by the journalist Seymour Hersh, published in November 1969 — including the shocking images taken by army photographer Ron Haeberle, who was present during the massacre to document the "body count" of Vietcong fighters — that instantly makes the crime known around the world. The horrified reaction to this article immediately leads to worldwide, massive, sustained protests against the war.

On February 1, 1968, the Saigon police chief shoots the 34-year-old Vietcong fighter Nguyen Van Lem in the open street.

1968 WEST GERMANY

the vietnam congress in berlin

Rudi Dutschke and the German revolution

After the murder of the student Benno Ohnesorg during the anti-Shah demonstration in West Berlin on June 2, 1967 (see page 120), the short heyday of the Socialist German Student Union (SDS) and its leader, Rudi Dutschke, begins in West Germany.

Since 1965, this left-wing champion at the Free University of Berlin has been railing against parliamentary democracy as representing elite interests and manipulating the people. He propagates a council republic, in which the people constitute the government. For Dutschke, Germany is just one of many places where the struggle for "liberation" must be fought. Whether in Germany, the USA, Vietnam, or Bolivia, direct democracy and a just society should be established in all places, and any form of foreign imperialism must be brought to an end. At the same time, the "German Che" considers gun violence to be legitimate in developing countries; developed countries, like Germany, should adhere to violence against objects.

National as well as international events fuel Dutschke's "anti-parliamentary utopia" and support a strong mobilization of those who want to put leftist theories into action. After the communist Tet Offensive challenges the U.S. military in Vietnam (see page 146) in January 1968, about 5,000 participants from all over the world, including the SDS, declare their solidarity with North Vietnam on February 17 and 18 at the International Vietnam Congress in West Berlin.

The conservative newspaper publisher, Axel Springer, is identified as a central domestic enemy and accused of baiting and manipulation. After Rudi Dutschke is injured in an assassination attempt on April 11, violence escalates during the "Easter riots" against the Springer corporation, which is accused of spiritual arson.

Activists see the country on its way to a "new fascism," especially after the grand coalition imposes so-called emergency laws in May 1968, regulating the powers of the executive in case of an extreme crisis. Anger is also directed against left-wing thinkers such as Theodor W. Adorno, with accusations that their anti-capitalist theories lack consequences.

Beginning in 1969, fierce tensions between radical and moderate members lead to the breakup of the SDS, which disbands in 1970. Despite their vociferousness, the radicals have always remained in the minority. Rudi Dutschke dies in 1979 from the after-effects of the assassination.

Around 5,000 congress participants call for solidarity with North Vietnam in February 1968. Standing at the podium is SDS leader Rudi Dutschke.

1968 USA

democratic convention in chicago

The Whole World is Watching

By the time the Democratic National Convention opened on August 26th, 1968 had already been one of the most violent years in a violent decade. The riots in Newark and Detroit had happened in July, Martin Luther King Jr. had been assassinated in April and Robert F. Kennedy, the most prominent anti-war candidate running for the Democratic nomination, had been assassinated in Los Angles in June. More than 16,000 Americans had been killed in Vietnam in 1968, the most of any year of the war.

The anger and division in the country had finally caused President Lyndon Johnson to admit that he could not win another election and declare that: "I shall not seek, and I will not accept, the nomination of my party for another term as your President." Against this background, the Democratic Convention in August was a referendum on the American political leadership's conduct of the war and its fitness to continue to lead.

Those who opposed the war were determined to make themselves heard both inside the convention hall and in the streets outside. Inside the convention, delegates who opposed the war were pushed, punched and shoved, and had their microphones turned off. Fights and shouting matches were broadcast on television. The protestors were met with such violence by the security guards inside the convention, that Walter Cronkite was moved to report to his television audience: "I think we've got a bunch of thugs here, if I may be permitted to say so." When the anti-war delegates demanded a vote on a "peace plank" and it was defeated, they marched around the convention hall singing "We Shall Overcome."

And things were much worse outside in the streets where thousands of anti-war demonstrators had converged on Chicago to disrupt the convention and make their voices heard. The scene was virtually a war zone. Mayor Daley, determined to prevent the protestors from reaching the convention, had amassed a force of 12,000 police, 7500 Army troops, 7500 Illinois National Guardsmen and 1000 Secret Service agents, armed with rifles, dogs and riot gear.

The protestors refused to be intimidated and returned again and again over the five-day convention to battle the police whose tactics were brutal. At one point the protestors, faced with repeated attacks by the police, began chanting "The whole world's watching," which was broadcast across the country.

Although it would still be years before the war in Vietnam was finally over, after Chicago the public appetite for the war and the political structure that supported it had been badly damaged. No longer could Johnson or any other President claim a broad consensus among the American people for a continuation of the war.

Delegates marched around the floor carrying 'Stop the War' signs and a huge black banner, protesting the majority decision to adopt the Johnson-Humphrey Administration policies on the war in Vietnam.

rage and disillusionment

Civil rights activists hit rock bottom

While the anti-Vietnam protest movement is still heading toward its climax in the USA, genuine student rebellion at U.S. universities has already passed its zenith. Civil rights activists are being heard by President Johnson, and a more just and democratic civil society seems to be on its way. Many activists start working from within the established system, while others propagate withdrawal from society and turn toward alternative ways of life.

Martin Luther King also becomes more confident and spiritual. On April 3, 1968, in a speech in Memphis, he asserts that he has seen "the Promised Land." The next day, he is shot dead on the balcony of the local Lorraine Motel by a white racist. His followers' mourning turns into rage; there are lootings and street fights in more than 100 cities, and whole rows of houses go up in flames as if in a bombing raid. Thirty-nine people lose their lives, 2,600 are injured, and 21,000 are arrested. On April 8, King's widow, Coretta, leads a peaceful protest march through Memphis. The next day, as many as 50,000 people join in the funeral procession.

The violence ends as abruptly as it began. Nevertheless, many black activists no longer believe in the possibility of a peaceful implementation of equal civil rights, and the divide between black and white increases. President Johnson seeks to calm the frustration by issuing another Civil Rights Act in April 1964, prohibiting discrimination against blacks in the purchase and renting of houses and apartments. But of course this is just a drop in the ocean.

Civil rights activists and liberals now turn their hopes to Robert Kennedy, who has already distinguished himself in the fight for civil rights as the U.S. attorney general under his brother's administration and is now running for president. He runs an unconventional and energetic election campaign, making himself the spokesman for many disadvantaged groups in society. He inspires great enthusiasm among African Americans and Latinos, and he wins several primaries. Following a speech delivered at the Ambassador Hotel in Los Angeles, he is shot dead by a Palestinian immigrant on the night of June 5, 1968 due to his "support for Israel" and he dies the next day. The whole country is in shock, and activists feel paralyzed. When the Republican Richard Nixon, known as a hardliner, wins the presidential election in November, many see it as a victory for the old system and an end to substantial change.

Two days after the murder of Martin Luther King, a whole block of streets in Chicago is reduced to rubble.

1968

marxism and communism

The theoretical foundation of the student revolution

They are a must at any demonstration: banners bearing the likenesses of Marx, Lenin, Mao, or Ho Chi Minh totter along like mascots and are gladly held up for the cameras (as, of course, is that of Che Guevara). Many student revolutionaries in Europe have a romantic, often even naïve admiration for communist movements and states in Asia and Latin America, which, however, is often due to their ignorance of the actual situation in those countries.

While they admire Mao's ideology for its support of guerrilla warfare and the liberation of the peasants (see page 116), North Vietnam's Ho Chi Minh is regarded as an ideal warrior against oppression and colonialism, both despite and because of his modest appearance. During the Vietnam War, he stands up to the U.S. imperialists. The fact that "Uncle Ho" also subjects his country to forced collectivization and strict cadre rule pales in comparison to his admirable popular education and literacy campaigns.

The more intellectual minds of the student movement are interested in Marx and Engels: Neo-Marxists try to compare Marxism's basic ideas with modern consumer and media society and thus produce highly theoretical, often unreadable pamphlets. Lenin is judged more critically, and the positive view of the October Revolution of 1917 contrasts with disappointment over Stalinist developments up to that time. Even Khrushchev's reforms cannot change that.

Students have a consistently positive attitude toward socialist ideals. On the other hand, they reject organized party communism, for which they are simply too anti-authoritarian, too activist, and too spontaneous. Realizing this, the communist parties of Europe (with the exception of the Italian PCI) do not support the students.

Nikita Khrushchev, Mao Tse-tung, and Ho Chi Minh at a banquet in Beijing.

1968 CZECHOSLOVAKIA

socialism with a human face

The rise and fall of the Prague Spring

Young people ride through the city center of Prague surrounded by a cheering crowd. They proudly wave the Czechoslovak national flag. During the spring and early summer months of 1968, the whole world is watching Czechoslovakia, because something unbelievable has been happening in this small Eastern Bloc country since the beginning of the year: The Communist Party is trying to build its own form of socialism under truly democratic conditions.

The hope of those who support "socialism with a human face" has a name: Alexander Dubček. After long internal party struggles, the Slovak reformer replaces the rigid dogmatist Antonin Novotny as First Secretary on 5 January and initiates a consistent social liberalization process, disregarding ideological taboos. He introduces reforms promoting economic and cultural pluralism: censorship is abolished, unions receive greater autonomy, and the opening of the economy and the strengthening of parliamentary rights

are announced. Furthermore, Stalinist crimes are to be uncovered and unjustly condemned citizens rehabilitated. The Communist Party's claim to leadership, however, is not at issue.

The vast majority of the population supports this path to liberalization "from above," and there are also many sympathizers in other Eastern Bloc countries (see pages 80 and 158). However, when euphoric intellectuals, artists, and athletes call for greater democratization in the "Two Thousand Words Manifesto," issued on June 27, the regime's response is reserved. From the beginning, the Soviets have suspiciously eyed the emancipation efforts of their wayward ally, and on July 3, for the first time, they ambiguously address the need for solidarity and unity among socialist countries. When Dubček refuses to back away from his reforms despite "friendly bilateral talks," something incredible happens again. On the night of August 20, Warsaw Pact

troops invade the country and pressure the regime to give in. The people of Prague struggle to resist the occupiers' tanks with their bare hands. Some are killed, and many are injured. Dubček is forced to resign in April 1969 and expelled from the Communist Party in 1970.

This abrupt end to a "Third Way" between socialism and capitalism undermines the ultimate moral legitimacy of the Soviet model of socialism, especially among those on the left.

Students sitting on Czechoslovak army trucks celebrate the reforms under Alexander Dubček on Wenceslas Square in Prague in the summer of 1968.

1968 POLAND

the polish march

The government represses the dissident movement

The student uprising in Poland in March 1968 is directly linked to developments in the USSR and Czechoslovakia. After Khrushchev has reckoned with Stalin's atrocities in February 1956, the head of the Polish Communist Party, Władysław Gomułka, who was elected after the Poznan riots in October, puts a stop to forced collectivization in his country, allows private companies to operate on a small scale, and modernizes the state economy. He also builds modern, prefabricated housing estates and improves the relationship between the state and the Catholic Church. His liberal measures provide Poland with a strong economic upswing until the mid-1960s and attract broad support.

Literary journals and discussion circles emerge during the cultural thaw, but the government soon curtails the newly granted cultural liberties. Inspired by the events of the Prague Spring (see page 156) and student protests in the West, Polish students rise up against these restrictions. In January 1968, the staging of the play *Forefathers' Eve* (1823–32) by the national poet Adam Mieckiewicz, which clearly expresses anti-Russian tendencies, sparks the rebellion. After students begin to pour into the performances, enthusiastically applauding the anti-Russian scenes and shouting "Independence without censorship!" and "Culture without censorship!", the play is banned. In March 1968, students who condemn the ban organize regular protest marches, which are immediately met with severe brutality from the authorities.

The suppression of the Polish student demonstrations coincides with an unprecedented anti-Semitic campaign in Europe. Interior Minister Mieczysław Moczar, who wants to replace Gomułka, denounces the student activists as "a Zionist fifth column" for supporting Israel during the Six-Day War and has them beaten up by pro-regime "citizens' militias" and "workers' rights activists." When the Polish Writer's Union sides with the students, a "war of leaflets and reports" breaks out, in which the international press also intervenes. But under the slogan "students to their studies, writers to their pens, Zionists to Zion," the Communist Party crushes the protests and, at the same time, forces 20,000 Polish Jews to emigrate.

Despite the ban on demonstrations and the restriction on recently gained freedoms, Poland is still in uproar. A renewed workers' uprising leads to the overthrow of Gomułka in late 1970. The continuity of the protest in Poland is also reflected in the fact that some of the protesters from 1968 will be the first supporters of Solidarnosc, fighting for the fall of communism in the 1980s.

On March 8, 1968, the military police attack and disperse a student demonstration in Warsaw.

1968

1968 TURKEY

student protests in turkey

Between Kemalism and revolution

The 1960s are a period of social upheaval in Turkey, in which student protest is one of the leading forces. Opposing the increasingly dictatorial, conservative Democratic Party, students organize massive protests and engage in violent confrontations with the authorities as early as 1960, because they see that the state doctrine — social reformist Kemalism — is in danger.

Influenced by Western student movements, students are demanding an "educational revolution," including the overthrow of the old university system, by the mid-1960s and also start to fight against imperialism and the U.S. presence in Turkey, which is a NATO ally.

From 1967 onward, the situation gets worse, but there are still different factions within the student body. For example, nationalist-Kemalist groups use the arrival of the U.S. Sixth Fleet in Istanbul in June as a reason for violent demonstrations against the "invaders," while the international-

ist-Marxist wing of the student movement organizes a protest march from Istanbul to Ankara in November 1967, demanding the nationalization of all private schools as well as the oil industry. The subsequent occupation of the University of Ankara in April 1968 finds imitators throughout the country.

However, the increasing propensity toward violence deprives leftist students of the previous support of the labor party, the TIP. This strengthens the nationalist wing of the student body, which is committed to a national revolutionary Kemalism.

After law enforcement officers raid a student dormitory and kill a student in Istanbul in July 1968, both wings join in a "National United Front," advocating violent actions and attacks on U.S. facilities, which lasts until 1969. The unrest peaks in Istanbul on February 16, 1969, also referred to as "Bloody Sunday," when right-wing paramilitary groups, including the "Gray Wolves,"

attack a march of students and unionists protesting the reanchoring of the U.S. Sixth Fleet in the Bosporus, killing two protesters and injuring 114.

The riots continue until the military intervenes in March 1971, banning left-wing groups and arresting leftist intellectuals, student leaders, and unionists.

Students from the Kemalist and Marxist student factions attack each other with batons in Ankara in 1968.

1968 ITALY

italy on its way to a popular uprising

Workers, students, and citizens join forces against the system

From the beginning, the '68 revolt is an alliance between workers and students, causing a political earthquake (compare this to France, page 164). The students understand themselves as part of the revolutionary workers' movement, even though their source of inspiration is not the union, but rather Che Guevara.

The revolt starts in northern Italy but eventually expands across the whole country. The north has experienced an enormous economic boom since the end of the 1950s, but wages and industrial relations law have remained unchanged. Furthermore, the universities still retain rigid authoritarian structures, against which the students now rise up.

On October 10, 1967, the day after Che's assassination (see page 132), students start to an occupation of the universities that will last for months. In March 1968, students and workers start violent street riots that continue into 1969, fighting the police and neo-fascist squads.

Many are injured or killed. The university students are supported by secondary school student committees, who occupy their own schools in solidarity.

In February 1968, independent trade unions are founded and call for mass strikes. Workers primarily occupy factories in the automobile and metal industries, bringing production to a standstill. At the end of 1968, the trade unions call for a general strike, 12 million workers across the country lay down their work, and the majority take to the streets. The protests culminate in the Battle at Corso Traiano in Turin on July 3, 1969, when a group demonstrating for the reform of the landlord-tenant law is brutally attacked by the police on their way to the Fiat plant, and citizens in the surrounding streets join forces with the demonstrators against the police.

By the end of 1969, the conflict has worsened: a series of devastating bomb attacks in railway stations, trains, and banks kill numerous innocent bystanders. The Italian government suspects

"left-wing anarchists." It takes until the 1980s to clarify that these acts of terror were committed by the neo-fascist terrorist organization Ordine Nuovo ("New Order"). Supported by right-wing extremists, the group follows a "strategy of tension": Out of fear of the left, the population is supposed to support an authoritarian, right-wing regime.

In 1970, the government finally puts an end to the workers' rebellion through wage increases, protection against unfair dismissal, and the long-contested right to form unions. The universities also undergo reforms, and the student riots die down.

However, individual radicals go underground, forming terrorist organizations like the Red Brigades. Left- and right-wing terrorist groups continue to commit kidnappings, killings, and bombings across Italy until the late 1980s.

Workers and students demonstrating in Rome in April 1968.

162

1968 FRANCE

"all power to the imagination!"

May 1968 in France

For a long time, French universities remain comparatively quiet. But in May 1968, French students achieve something that has not happened anywhere else: they mobilize the population and put the government in a tight spot.

The protests come from a group of left-anarchist students, headed by Daniel Cohn-Bendit, at the suburban Nanterre University, and reach the Sorbonne University in Paris on May 3. After the violent termination of protest activities and the closure of the Sorbonne, the unrest spreads to the Latin Quarter, where demonstrators are entrenched behind barricades.

The brutal dissolution of the blockades on the night of May 11 continues to escalate the situation. Important French labor unions spontaneously declare their solidarity with the concerns of the student movement and call for a general strike. One year earlier, scattered work stoppages had already taken place in France, but now there is a seething unrest throughout the country. Even the willingness of the government, under President Georges Pompidou, to defer to the students' demands does not ease the situation. On the contrary, the protesters feel strengthened and now demand not only the democratization of the university, but of all sectors of society. Five hundred thousand people take to the streets in Paris on May 13, along with tens of thousands across the country — and it is clear to all of France that this mass demonstration is a political reckoning with the Fifth Republic under President General de Gaulle.

Once again there are work stoppages and factory occupations. At times, up to nine million workers are on strike. Students' and artists' appeals and graffiti around the Sorbonne bear witness to the spirit of rebellion: "Long live the commune!" "Sabotage the culture industry [...] Reinvent life!" "All power to the imagination!"

But these dreams soon fail in real life: when de Gaulle calls for new parliamentary elections in a speech on May 30, the rebellion collapses as quickly as it had arisen. Workers go back to work, and university life slowly returns to normal. The fragmented left withdraws into its own circles. In the June 1968 elections, the Gaullists win a clear victory.

Students throw stones at French policemen on May 3, 1968, during a street fight in Paris.

1968

rebellion in the peaceful north

Swedish students rise up

In May 1968, the small town of Båstad in southwestern Sweden is in an uproar. During an international tennis tournament, a confrontation takes place between the police and demonstrators protesting the participation of the apartheid state Rhodesia. Although the result is merely minor injuries and soiled police uniforms, the media speaks of the worst outburst of violence in recent history. In particular, the Social Democratic newspaper *Arbetarbladet* deplores this "un-Swedish behavior." Violence and street riots are imports that have nothing to do with Swedish democracy, because the country has virtually unlimited freedom to demonstrate.

The conflicts in Sweden — as well as in Norway and Denmark — are not as radical as those in most other European countries due to the unique integrating power of the political system: social liberal parties have governed Scandinavia since the 1930s. There is a broad social consensus that the state is responsible for stability and balance between class differences, and that economic growth should not only serve a wealthy upper class, but should primarily further the common good.

In the turbulent 1960s, the Swedish government relies on understanding rather than aggressive confrontation. The police take a relatively defensive approach. There are hardly any attacks against protesters. Therefore, excessive street battles do not take place and — in contrast to France and Germany — the state does not become the enemy.

Nevertheless, the Vietnam War upsets the Swedish public. Groups form throughout the country, agitating against the imperialist U.S. war and linking this protest to a leftist upheaval in Sweden. By the end of the 1960s, the number of coalitions actively canvassing popular support has risen to well over 100. Particularly in Stockholm and Lund, but also in other parts of the country, demonstrations are taking place, texts are being published, and protest groups are gathering in front of U.S. facilities. And again, the Swedish government goes along with it: as a Western head of government, Prime Minister Olof Palme (see page 184) criticizes U.S. policy in Vietnam with unusual sharpness. Thus the state also takes the wind out of the sails of leftist revolutionaries in this matter.

Protest against the International Monetary Fund on March 29, 1968, in Stockholm.

1968

1968 MAURITIUS

a triumph of multiculturalism

Mauritius gains independence

While ethnic and tribal conflicts plunge many of Africa's independent states into violent conflicts in the 1960s (see page 10), the island of Mauritius, east of Madagascar, manages a remarkably peaceful transition despite its strong multiethnic diversity.

During Portuguese, Dutch, French, and British colonial rule, diverse ethnic groups came to the island. Ruling the country from 1810 onward, the British created huge sugar cane plantations, and after the abolition of slavery, they brought many Hindus and Muslims from India to work as indentured laborers, who soon formed the majority of the population.

Since 1965, the British and a large party alliance from various ethnic groups, under the leadership of the Socialist Workers Party, have been preparing for Mauritius's independence, which is proclaimed after the passing of a new constitution in March 1968. The harmonizing socialist leader Sir Seewoosagur Ramgoolam, also known as the "Father of the Nation," wins the free,

multi-party elections and serves as the country's first prime minister, with different coalitions, until 1982. Mauritius is part of the Commonwealth until 1992, when it becomes a republic. The slow transition works: despite some difficulties, the island state is stable even today, with the highest average life expectancy of all sub-Saharan countries.

The state is a remarkable example of successful multiethnic diversity. The 1967 Constitution explicitly grants equal civil rights as well as equal opportunities to all ethnic groups and defines multiculturalism or multiethnicity as the basis of society. At the time, two-thirds of the Mauritian population is Indo-Mauritian, culturally and religiously consisting of Hindu, Tamil, Telugu, Marathi, and Muslim people. About 27% are Creole — descendants of black slaves from Madagascar — and minorities of Sino-Mauritians of Chinese origin and white Franco-Mauritians each make up about three percent of the population. Each of these groups

has its own advocates, but ethnic identity largely plays a minor role. The voting system, however, fosters the proportional representation of ethnic groups in parliament.

Initially, the integration of the Creoles, whose culture and language has long been seen as a lower-class phenomenon and a remnant of French slavery, proves difficult. In 1969, activists form a Marxist Creole party inspired by the student revolt in France, which quickly gains political relevance, ensuring that Creole is valued as an important aspect of identity in Mauritanian society.

Women supporting the Mauritanian prime minister in a demonstration held in London in 1967.

1968 BRAZIL

the march of the one hundred thousand

Riots against the military regime in Brazil

Tensions boil over when the military police in Rio de Janeiro kill the teenage student Edson Luís de Lima Souto on the university campus during a student protest on March 28, 1968: the anger and frustration students feel over the authoritarian social conditions crippling the country for the last four years sparks explosive outbursts of violence in Rio, Brasília, and São Paulo.

In 1964, a military junta, supported by the CIA, had seized control of the government and curtailed basic civil rights. The regime's plan for repressive university reform, aimed at streamlining the curriculum and cutting politically controversial programs of study, gives rise to initially peaceful but ineffective student demonstrations.

But the first death of a student activist at the hands of the military government leads to spontaneous public solidarity with the student movement: nearly 50,000 mourners, including many artists and intellectuals, turn the funeral into a political demonstration demanding more democracy in Brazil. On an almost daily basis, further protests against the regime are held in university towns across the country. The demonstrators not only demand academic freedom, but also the abolition of censorship and the end of arbitrary public repression.

Inspired by these events, radical leftists organize the first worker's strikes. But the state takes harsh measures, the police break up every riot, and there are countless casualties, arrests, and further deaths. The uprising against the violent military regime culminates in the "March of the One Hundred Thousand" through Rio de Janeiro on June 26, 1968. Arranged as a deliberately non-violent mass demonstration, the march proceeds largely peacefully — and without any political success. On the contrary, the regime uses this incident and the turmoil of the months leading up to it to justify strengthening authoritarian control. The president dissolves Congress at the end of the year, public political gatherings are forbidden, and any kind of opposition is brutally suppressed. Several left-wing students follow the example of the guerrilla warrior Che Guevara and opt for armed struggle, which only leads to further deaths. It will take Brazil another 20 years to return to full democracy.

Following the funeral of Edson Luís de Lima Souto on April 4, 1968, mounted police officers use batons and sabers to disperse a crowd of demonstrators in Rio de Janeiro.

1968 MEXICO

the massacre of tlatelolco

The student death toll

Between 1929 and 2000, the Institutional Revolutionary Party (PRI) rules Mexico. Until the 1960s, the ruling party's combination of planned and market economies spurs great economic growth, with rapid expansion of heavy and consumer goods industries. Mexico shifts from an agrarian to an industrial nation, increasing its industrialization by 240% (this comes to be known as "the Mexican miracle").

As a downside, the PRI's patronage system penetrates all areas of society, linking any advancement to membership in or proximity to the party. The opposition is harassed, and the PRI bribes rural peasants with food and building materials before the elections and carts them to the polls. The PRI controls the elections: ballot boxes disappear and dead people "vote" for the state party.

In 1968, Mexico City invests $150 million in preparation for hosting the 19th Olympic Games, which are taking place in a developing country for the very first time. Students from the National Autonomous University of Mexico (UNAM) and other universities see this as an opportunity to capture the world's attention and demonstrate for cultural and academic freedom.

Following the brutal suppression of the first protests, 70 university delegations found a National Strike Committee and demand the release of all political prisoners. On August 1, 1968, the rector of UNAM leads a protest of 50,000 students against government repression. They occupy the campus of the Polytechnic Institute and are joined by the students there. Approximately 500 students are injured in street fights. In mid-September, nearly half a million people participate in a silent march through the inner city.

Then, on October 2, 1968, ten days before the opening of the "Games of Peace," 10,000 students and numerous citizens gather for a peaceful protest in the Square of the Three Cultures in the Tlatelolco district of Mexico City. While listening to the speakers, they are fired upon by snipers on the rooftops of the surrounding houses and by military tanks. The protesters panic and flee into neighboring streets or seek cover in doorways. But the assault leaves about 300 dead and countless injured in the square. Over 3,000 students are arrested. The PRI officially reports 20 dead and prevents any further investigation of the massacre. After PRI rule finally comes to an end in 2001, previously classified documents eventually reveal that the gunmen were members of the presidential guard and the secret police.

Demonstrators flee from gunfire and tear gas on the Square of the Three Cultures on October 2, 1968.

1968

1968 SOVIET UNION

the gulag archipelago

Reckoning with the Soviet labor camp system

Aleksandr Solzhenitsyn was not only the most knowledgeable chronicler of the Soviet forced labor camp system, he was also one of its most prominent victims.

As early as 1918, the Soviet leadership began to establish prison camps, which Stalin expanded into a network of labor camps and special settlements for exiles. At least 18 million people were interned in such facilities between 1930 and 1953; up to 32 million were conscripted into forced labor. The prisoners were assigned to hard labor in sewers, on railways, and in industrial construction, and the death toll was high. The camp and settlement system forms its own sphere within the Soviet-Russian state, namely the "Gulag Archipelago" — Gulag is the Russian abbreviation for the Headquarters of Corrective Labor Camps and Colonies.

As a Red Army soldier, Sol-zhenitsyn participates in several major battles during the Second World War. Shortly before the end of the war, he is arrested for writing a letter in which he criticizes Stalin from a Leninist perspective. He is sentenced to eight years of forced labor at a special camp for scientists and recounts his experiences in his novel *The First Circle* (1968). Suffering from cancer, the author is released in 1953 but is "banished for life" to a desolate settlement in Kazakhstan. Dismissed in 1957, he publishes his first story about the Gulag in 1962 ("One Day in the Life of Ivan Denisovich"). Still under observation, he continues to write secretly. The KGB seizes his manuscripts several times. He completes his masterpiece, *The Gulag Archipelago*, in 1968, which is published in the West in late 1973 and circulated in the Russian underground. Consequently, Solzhenitsyn is expelled from the Soviet Union in 1974.

As one of the most influential books of the 20th century, *The Gulag Archipelago* meticulously describes the structure and economic relevance of the Soviet "prison industry," the constant influx of new inmates, and their deaths from hard labor and malnutrition.

Solzhenitsyn's works from 1962 to 1968, for which he is awarded the Nobel Prize for Literature in 1970, are immediately published in the West, sparking discussions among leftists and communists. His ruthless depiction of Stalin's perfidious surveillance and punishment system in *The First Circle* eventually has a significant influence on Western students: Soviet and other Eastern Bloc real-socialist models (except for the Prague Spring) are now dismissed in debates about systemic change or seen as cautionary tales about the suppression of freedom.

Aleksandr Solzhenitsyn arrives in Zurich after his expulsion from the Soviet Union.

1968

"we all live in a yellow submarine"

A psychedelic pop fairy tale

Only the Beatles can help. An army of nasty, music-hating Blue Meanies is attacking the cheerful inhabitants of Pepperland. After successfully overcoming many dangers on their way, Sgt. Pepper's Lonely Hearts Club Band finally manages to reach the promised Pepperland in a yellow submarine and chase away the Blue Meanies — with their music. This unique pop movie clearly conveys a hippie, albeit somewhat simplistic, view of the world. The good guys have the colors, the love, and the music. In contrast, those who have no colors, no imagination, and only give orders are the bad guys.

The third and final Beatles movie, after *A Hard Day's Night* (1964) and *Help!* (1965), reflects the naïve, utopian hopes of its generation in such a playful and creative way that it is nowadays considered a cinematic masterpiece of its time — particularly because it was so different. For the first time, a cartoon — previously the domain of infantile Walt Disney movies — also addresses an adult audience with style and complexity. Furthermore, it is the band's first animated feature, with the live-action Beatles only making their appearance in the closing scene. Instead, great Beatles songs such as "Nowhere Man" and "Lucy in the Sky with Diamonds" are brilliantly translated into psychedelic visuals. This animated film is also a groundbreaking contemporary video clip from the Beatles' most creative period.

However, the film project seems difficult in the beginning. The Canadian director George Dunning supervises 200 artistic collaborators working in London studios day and night. Right up to the end, there is no real script. In an interview, the film's art director, Heinz Edelmann, describes *Yellow Submarine* as one of the most chaotic productions in film history. The long-time illustrator for the German youth magazine *twen* is the creative mastermind behind the surreal, colorful images. In the end, even the initially skeptical Beatles are satisfied. Premiering in London on July 17, 1968, *Yellow Submarine* becomes their most successful movie — and a milestone in terms of design and pop aesthetics.

Poster artwork by Heinz Edelmann for the movie Yellow Submarine.

subversive revolutionaries

Students and Kabouters engage in politics

In May 1969, a year after the great unrest in Paris, there are also riots at Dutch universities: students occupy the universities of Tilburg, Leiden, Amsterdam, and other cities. They demand higher scholarships and affordable housing and protest against the privatization of teaching programs. Over the course of the lengthy conflicts with the university administrations, the students extend their demands: the Dutch university system must become more democratic, and student councils must be involved in administrative and academic decisions.

What seems utopian at first actually comes to pass: most of the professors join the student revolt, creating a strong and successful alliance between the student body and the faculty. In 1970, a liberal university law eliminates both the old, undemocratic, hierarchical structures and the originally intended privatization.

There are good reasons why the student protests do not turn into riots and are much less politically charged compared to those in other countries. Despite the country's set social structures and the four "pillars of society" (the state-supporting Calvinist, the Catholic, the liberal, and the socialist sphere) all existing side by side — with their own parties, organizations, newspapers, and schools — there is a stronger feeling of consensus in the Netherlands than elsewhere. In addition, tendencies have been noticeable since the mid-1960s. The disrespectful activities of the Provo Movement (see page 98), for example, have helped break down conventions and supported the founding of new political parties of all persuasions, without confessional barriers. Beginning in the mid-1960s, Dutch society modernizes itself and becomes one of the most liberal societies in Europe in the 1970s.

In 1969, the Kabouters ("goblins") are founded in Amsterdam as an offshoot of the Provo Movement, giving fresh impetus to other alternative cultures across Europe. In October 1969, they introduce their plan for an "Amsterdam Kabouter City" to the city council. The plan aims to reconcile human beings with nature and to resist pollution and the terror of consumerism. The Kabouters open up organic stores, selling homegrown produce, and barter markets to combat the throwaway culture. Kabouter groups form in more than 60 cities. In 1970, the Kabouters are elected to the Amsterdam City Parliament. Thus the anarchists themselves now carry political responsibility.

Students run during a protest in Amsterdam.

1969

1969 USA

the birth of gay pride

The LGBT community fights back in the Stonewall Riots

New York City, June 28, 1969. At around 2:15 a.m. all hell breaks loose in front of the Stonewall Inn, the gay and transgender bar on Christopher Street in Manhattan: several police units arrive to free their colleagues, who have been trapped by an angry mob inside the bar, in which they started a raid an hour earlier. What has happened?

Homosexuality is defined as a mental illness in the U.S. at the time (and even until 1973). Public kissing and private sex between gay or lesbian partners are criminalized in most states, and the FBI keeps lists and monitors identified homosexuals. It is not until 1966 that provocative activities undertaken by the Mattachine Society, the first gay rights organization in the U.S., manage to lift the prohibition against serving alcohol to gay people in bars. Consequently, numerous bars open, now focusing on a gay clientele. Nevertheless, gay bars and nightclubs in New York frequently face raids by the police, who check identification and make arrests.

This being the case, it is not unusual that four police officers enter the Stonewall Inn on June 28 for a raid. But things get out of hand when the police start harassing men in women's clothing, and several people refuse to show their identification. People gather from nearby pubs and from the park across the street, and the reaction to the police grows hostile. When the police try to take the people they have arrested away, the first stones and bottles are thrown at the patrol wagon. Protesters try to set fire to the bar and chant "gay power." The crowd swells to 2,000 people, confronted by 400 police officers after backup has arrived. Chaotic scenes follow, but eventually the police manage to disperse the crowd at around four in the morning. Some are injured, and there is severe property damage but no deaths. The protests continue the following night, but less violently.

The courage of the protesters, who resisted and refused to endure harassment passively, gives the homosexual and transgender movement a tremendous boost in the U.S. and around the world. The Gay Pride movement emerges and publicly advocates for gay rights. On June 28, 1970, the movement organizes a memorial march with 10,000 participants, thus establishing the tradition of today's Gay Pride parades in many countries.

Scene from the movie Stonewall *by Roland Emmerich (2015).*

1969 USA

woodstock

A chaotic music festival becomes a legend

The mythologization of the three-day open-air festival has already begun the day after it ends: on August 18, 1969, a feature article in the *New York Times* reports on an extraordinary festival, which has proceeded peacefully despite adverse circumstances, in contrast to similar events. In the same year, the political activist Abbie Hoffman's book on *The Woodstock Nation* embodies that other, peaceful, better America. But most of all, it is the spectacular three-hour music documentary film about Woodstock, released a year later, that brings the saga of the most important music festival of the Peace and Love generation to the world. In this way, the performances of Janis Joplin, Jimi Hendrix, and Joe Cocker become world famous. Nowadays, Woodstock is synonymous with the wild, free, ecstatic community spirit of the 1960s. In reality, the festival was planned quite differently — and almost everything went wrong.

Initially, the Woodstock Music & Art Fair is not evidence of a yearning for a better world, but a rather profane advertising idea. To promote the opening of a music studio in Woodstock, the music managers Michael Lang and Artie Kornfeld start organizing a spectacular concert for 200,000 people in February 1969. They hire famous musicians, pay substantial fees, and finally identify a 600-acre farm area near Bethel in New York State as a seemingly suitable venue. However, more than twice that many people crowd the premises, turning the festival into an organizational disaster. Everything is missing: security personnel, sanitary facilities, food, and water tanks. Cars create a traffic jam for miles. Festival attendees overrun the entrances. In addition, torrential thunderstorms destroy parts of the structures and transform the place into a mudhole. Two people die during the event — one from an overdose, another run over by a tractor. Yet, considering the sheer numbers and the lack of control, there are comparatively few accidents or violent outbreaks.

Undoubtedly, the unintentionally chaotic organization has added to the festival's air of imperfection and anarchy and given rise to the Woodstock myth. The festival ends in an economic fiasco for the organizers and retrospectively marks the spectacular end of the hippie movement.

A rain break during the Woodstock festival.

olof palme: socialist and world politician

A visionary becomes prime minister

Earlier than other Western European countries, Sweden is already on its way to becoming a liberal, modern society. For 23 years, from 1946 to 1969, the Social Democrat Tage Erlander governs the country and establishes the Swedish welfare state, which offers its citizens unique social benefits to this day. His goal is a "strong society," in which particularly strong social provisioning should stimulate the self-reliant engagement of its citizens. The "Swedish model" attracts worldwide attention.

In 1953, Olof Palme becomes Erlander's personal secretary, then his political advisor, and finally a cabinet minister. He implements groundbreaking reforms, such as gender equality in the workplace and in taxation, as well as the right to childcare. In February 1968, he provokes an international political scandal: as a Swedish cabinet minister, he demonstrates against the Vietnam War alongside the North Vietnamese ambassador in Moscow. As a consequence,

the U.S. withdraws their ambassador from Stockholm. All at once, Palme becomes internationally famous and embodies the charismatic hope of the reformist left.

After the Social Democrats win more than 50% of the popular vote in the 1968 elections, Erlander steps down and is succeeded by his 42-year-old friend Olof Palme as the Social Democratic party leader and the head of state in October 1969. As prime minister of a non-revolutionary socialist system, he embodies a new type: youthful radiance paired with an educated, middle-class background, unbridled faith in progress, and reformist impatience with any kind of social standstill. At the international level, he consistently protests against the Vietnam War and every other war, frequently offering his services as a mediator. His support for nuclear energy as a way to reduce global warming and his proposal for a nuclear-weapons-free corridor

in Europe make him popular beyond the borders of Sweden. In general, Palme thinks not only in national categories, but also on a global level: together with German Chancellor Willy Brandt and Austrian Chancellor Bruno Kreisky, Palme initiates the North-South Dialogue against poverty in the Southern Hemisphere. All three are concerned about world peace and an equitable global distribution of resources.

Domestically, however, Palme is unable to maintain Erlander's success. In 1976, his government is voted out of office. Palme returns as prime minister in 1982, but on February 28, 1986, he is shot dead in the street in Stockholm. The case remains unsolved, with sloppy investigations nourishing conspiracy theories to this day.

Olof Palme spontaneously jumps onto a pile of foam rubber while visiting an art exhibition at the Moderna Museet in Stockholm in 1968.

1969

1969 CHILE

a socialist experiment

Salvador Allende reforms Chile and provokes a deadly coup

Dreaming of a freely elected socialism rooted among the people, the international left looks to Chile at the end of the 1960s, where the charismatic and politically experienced socialist Salvador Allende is running for office in the upcoming parliamentary elections.

For years, there have been severe conflicts within the Chilean government. Prevailing against the strong political right, the Christian Democrats enforce the nationalization of copper mining, the formation of free trade unions, and the first land reform in Chile. Yet in 1965, the extreme right and the extreme left start a guerrilla war in which the Christian Democrats, who are too "communist" for the right and too conservative for the left, are caught in the middle.

In 1969, the Christian Left, the socialists, and the communists — including seven smaller Marxist parties — found the Unidad Popular (Popular Unity Party). Their 40-point action program calls for radical social reforms, and their candidate is Salvador Allende, who actually scores a (narrow) victory over the united right-wing conservatives the following year. This victory of a popular front in free elections sends a welcome signal to the international left, and Allende receives sympathy and support from around the world. He immediately implements radical improvements for the lower classes, increasing wages by up to 60%, nationalizing mineral resources, and enforcing land reform for the benefit of the peasants. Education, school meals, and healthcare will be provided free of charge.

But his next step will have fatal consequences: when he expropriates U.S. copper mining companies with the consent of all parties, the U.S. cuts off economic aid and imposes a boycott. Chile's foreign debt reaches astronomical heights, and printing new money raises inflation by more than 300%.

Seeing Chile on a path toward communism, the U.S. wages targeted destabilization campaigns. The CIA finances right-wing terrorist groups and assassination attempts. By 1973, right-wing guerrillas have perpetrated over 600 terrorist attacks. Public order is threatened, and Allende is forced to declare a state of emergency. He wants to resolve the constitutional crisis with a democratic plebiscite. But before he is able to announce this plan, a junta of right-wing generals under Augusto Pinochet, aided by the U.S., deposes the government on September 11, 1973. Allende is killed in the coup. The socialist experiment has failed, and Chile descends into dictatorship.

Salvador Allende greets workers at a factory.

1969

1969 USA

the climax of the anti-vietnam protest

The movement reaches the middle class

Under Richard Nixon everything would be different in Vietnam. He leads his presidential campaign in 1968 with the promise to end the war in Vietnam. As President, he speaks of the goal of "Vietnamization" in June 1969, which implies the withdrawal of U.S. soldiers. However, an end to the war in Nixon's understanding can only mean a victory for the United States. From this perspective, Nixon is willing to expand the war if North Vietnam refuses to respond to U.S. demands. If there is any doubt, the war should be intensified by all means. He even briefly considers the use of nuclear weapons.

The population's resistance against the war, however, continues to grow, especially after the details of the My Lai massacre (see page 146) come to light in June: on March 16, 1968, U.S. soldiers brutally murdered around 500 defenseless villagers, many of them women and children. The government's assertion that the war is being fought to defend freedom and democracy in Vietnam loses any tangible connection with reality.

In the fall of 1969, opponents of the war have mobilized like never before. Even though predominantly left-wing groups organize the rallies, most participants do not wish to criticize society in principle, but want to see an end to U.S. involvement in Southeast Asia. On October 15, 250,000 people attend the largest demonstration against the Vietnam War in Washington, DC.

Throughout the country, workers regularly lay down their tools to demonstrate against the killing in Vietnam. Even high-ranking politicians speak up against official U.S. policy. In New York, Mayor John Lindsay proclaims a day of mourning with flags flown at half-mast. At Trinity Church in the heart of the city, citizens read out the names of those who have been killed in Vietnam — nearly 40,000. In North Newton, activists ring an ancient bell, tolling once for every dead soldier.

Nixon is hardly impressed by the actions and rallies across the nation in October and November 1969, speaking instead of a "noisy minority." When the president extends the war into Cambodia in 1970, the protests become more radical, as does the retaliation of law enforcement agencies. During a mass protest on the Kent State University campus on May 4, 1970, four students are shot dead by the Ohio National Guard. Two days later, two more students are killed in Mississippi. The fight against the war threatens to become a civil war in itself. And yet the Vietnam War continues until 1975.

Lecturers from Harvard Medical School collect signatures against the Vietnam War in Boston in October 1969.

the american indian movement

Native Americans raise their voices

In the 1960s, living conditions on Native American reservations in the U.S. have already been disastrous for decades: fleeced and deceived by corrupt reservation administrations, many Natives are subjected to illiteracy and unemployment, domestic violence and heavy alcoholism. Laws prohibit them from seeking employment in the cities.

The civil rights movement also stirs up indigenous activists, who are encouraged by Martin Luther King and Robert Kennedy.

In the early 1960s, the American Indian writer Jack D. Forbes organizes the first individual protests. As co-founder of the Tribal College Movement in 1966, he manages to establish tribal colleges on the reservations. The movement also establishes Quetzalcoatl University in California, which allows American Indians to pursue a college degree in modern science while taking their own traditions and values into account.

In 1968, around 250 activists found the American Indian Movement (AIM) in Minneapolis as a political advocacy group for all Indian tribes. AIM strongly models its tactics on those of the Black Panthers (see page 112). Together, they lead the Rainbow Coalition of radical civil rights groups. The movement organizes indigenous self-help groups, provides legal aid, and primarily initiates symbolic acts of civil disobedience to publicly express its concerns.

In November 1969, members of several tribes and leaders of AIM occupy the deserted prison island of Alcatraz, referring to an earlier treaty that identified any unused federal land available for Indian use. In 1970, AIM activists gather at Mount Rushmore to raise awareness of the fact that the national monument's four presidents' heads are located on Sioux territory, which was unlawfully expropriated in the nineteenth century.

In the early 1970s, AIM organizes other spectacular actions, such as the Trail of Broken Treaties, with the storming of the Bureau of Indian Affairs in Washington, DC in 1972 and the occupation of Wounded Knee village on the South Dakota Pine Ridge Reservation in 1973, which ends violently.

All of these media-savvy activities help raise awareness of Native American cultural heritage and improve the advancement of indigenous people. However, even today, they continue to be disadvantaged and marginalized.

On November 20, 1969, 89 Native Americans occupy the former prison island of Alcatraz off the coast of San Francisco, intending to build an Indian Cultural Center, including a university. The U.S. government is initially willing to negotiate, but finally clears the island in 1971.

"give peace a chance"

Conscientious objectors support the peace movement

"All we are saying is give peace a chance." John Lennon records this song with Yoko Ono on June 1, 1969, in Montreal during a so-called "bed-in." The newlywed couple gives interviews from their bed, using their publicity to promote their "Campaign for Peace."

The song becomes the musical anthem of the international peace movement, which mostly draws its increasing strength from the protest against the Vietnam War, but ultimately goes far beyond it. "Make love, not war" is the catchy slogan for a pacifist utopia, according to which peace is more than just the absence of military conflict. It is necessary to overcome a culture based on violence and exploitation. According to pacifist principles, all existing ideologies and ways of life are to be eliminated in favor of a peaceful, equal coexistence without coercion or structural violence.

This alternative model to the militant present is also reflected in the musical *Hair*, which premieres on Broadway in 1968, becoming one of the most successful and powerful pop culture performances of its kind. Catchy song-and-dance scenes capture the tragic story Claude Hooper Bukowski, a farm boy from Oklahoma, who is torn between his pacifist ideals and his supposed patriotic duty to fight for his country in Vietnam.

Unlike Bukowski, many hippies act according to their convictions and refuse to perform military service. The more people become aware of the brutality of the war in Southeast Asia, the more resistance grows in the U.S. Young men are publicly burning their draft cards, and many decide to flee to neighboring Canada or to Europe. Soldiers who have already been drafted desert the military.

In an attempt to undermine the burgeoning anti-war movement, President Nixon finally ends the draft in 1973.

His successor, Gerald Ford, seeks social reconciliation and offers conditional amnesty to approximately 50,000 deserters and conscientious objectors who face charges at home and are hiding abroad.

Illustration for the magazine Eye, *c. 1969.*

one giant leap for mankind

The first man walks on the moon

On July 21, 1969, millions of people around the world are holding their breath in front of their televisions and radios. Then, finally, comes the announcement: "Houston, Tranquility Base here. The Eagle has landed." Then six long hours and 40 minutes pass before the astronaut Neil Armstrong cautiously descends the ladder. As the first person to step on the powdery surface of the moon, he writes human history with his words: "That's one small step for a man, one giant leap for mankind."

For over two and a half hours, Armstrong and Buzz Aldrin carefully walk across the unknown terrain, taking rock samples, placing measuring instruments, and ramming the U.S. flag into the ground. The 600 million TV viewers should see that the Americans are the first to land on the moon.

The successful mission is not only a groundbreaking technical achievement, transgressing the boundaries of the known human habitat, but above all a victory over the Soviet Union in the long-running race to supremacy in space. It is a political and technological triumph in the Cold War and a balm for the soul of a nation experiencing a moral and military disaster in Vietnam.

Until the moon landing, the Soviet Union, which aims to prove the technological superiority of socialism through ambitious space programs, has always been one step ahead of the U.S. On October 4, 1957, the Russians succeed in sending the first satellite, Sputnik 1, into orbit, and on April 12, 1961, Yuri Gagarin becomes the first man to orbit the earth (see page 24). In the early summer of 1961, few people believe in the feasibility of President Kennedy's goal "of landing a man on the moon and returning him safely to the earth" by the late 1960s.

The humiliation is so great for the Soviet Union that the landing of the U.S. astronauts is not broadcast live on Soviet television. Neither do the Chinese receive any real-time reports.

The political power of the images and the pinpoint accuracy of the mission quickly gives rise to the belief that the moon landing was staged in a film studio. Despite all objective scientific evidence, this conspiracy theory continues to this day.

In reality, the meaning of the moon landing is mainly symbolic. Even today, it still stands for the ability of human beings to change their fate and the world in which they live — and therefore it is also a symbolic highlight of the 1960s.

The first man on the moon — a moving event in the collective memory of humanity to this day.

1969

EPILOGUE

The optimism of the sixties *is fueled by the confidence in humankind's ability to improve living conditions, society, and the world. This positive attitude can be found almost everywhere in the world among the younger generation, although it is expressed very differently in different countries. Protest against the establishment does not end abruptly in 1969, but continues into the 1970s. Many initiatives from the 1960s have medium- and long-term effects, and social discourse takes on new, more democratic forms in the West that would not have been possible without the revolts of the 1960s.*

The end of great utopias

A characteristic of the protest movement in the Western world in the late 1960s is the dwindling belief in rapid societal and political change. The worldwide revolution — insofar as it is worth striving for — does not take place. Many activists now turn their backs on grand social utopias and focus on more concrete issues and closer targets. They organize resistance and change in their own environments. On the one hand, this change from the visionary to the pragmatic has much to do with experiences drawn from the 1960s and with disillusionment in the face of progress that is just too small and too slow for radical reformers. On the other hand, this "downsizing" corresponds to the feeling of economic insecurity in the early 1970s. Whereas the 1960s were marked by high economic growth, full employment, and a belief in technological progress, a prevailing sense of crisis is now emerging in Western industrialized countries. The oil crisis of 1973 causes a sharp recession, accompanied by mass unemployment and the gradual disintegration of traditional industrial structures, reinforced by increasing competitive pressure from low-

wage Asian countries. The Club of Rome already speaks of the "end of growth" in 1972, thereby raising awareness of the limitations of natural resources. Environmental issues are also becoming more important.

Against this backdrop, the protest movement of the '68 generation falls into three groups: the dropouts, the reformers, and the radicals. Disillusioned dropouts turn away from sociopolitical commitment and pursue personal projects instead — either as individualists in civil society or in autonomous communes, such as in the Christiania settlement in Copenhagen, founded in 1971. Those who continue to believe in the reformability of established society set out to "work from within the system," going into politics, administration, or even the cultural sector. And the few political deserters and radical idealists who believe in starting a revolution by force go underground. So the terrorism of the 1970s through 1990s is a direct consequence of the 1960s. While the Palestine Liberation Organization (PLO) aims at drawing attention to the precarious situation of the Palestinians with attacks such as the Munich massacre during

Anti-nuclear protesters demonstrate in front of a nuclear power plant.

taken by the state, which provoke fierce public discussions, constitutional standards are largely retained in these two young democracies.

The legacy

As a long-term effect of the rise of freedom in the 1960s, the Western world experiences a wave of social liberation in the 1970s: civil rights are strengthened, social equality is promoted, education systems become more permeable and universities more democratic, and employee participation rights are sustained.

Protest structures from the 1960s spark many new movements that turn public attention to specific concerns — such as environmental protection, the responsible use of nuclear power, women's equality, and securing peace. Direct democratic initiative groups emerge and mobilize citizens "from below." This change in values — toward self-determination and self-realization — facilitates the increasing individualization of life plans. In the dictatorial East, however, individualization is suppressed, but becomes all the more effective in later years.

Christoph Marx

the Olympic Games in 1972, European left-wing terrorists, especially in Germany and Italy, see themselves as avant-garde pioneers of the working class. Partially backed by the PLO, the German Red Army Faction (RAF) and the Italian Red Brigades work to destabilize the state with attacks, murders, and kidnappings, but they fail in the end. Despite rigid control measures

INDEX

PHOTO CREDITS

The pictures were provided courtesy of

COPYRIGHT